—African-American Biographies—

MAHALIA JACKSON

The Voice of Gospel and Civil Rights

Series Consultant:
Dr. Russell L. Adams, Chairman
Department of Afro-American Studies, Howard University

Barbara Kramer

Enslow Publishers, Inc.
40 Industrial Road   PO Box 38
Box 398   Aldershot
Berkeley Heights, NJ 07922   Hants GU12 6BP
USA   UK
http://www.enslow.com

Library of Congress Cataloging-in-Publication Data

Kramer, Barbara.
  Mahalia Jackson : the voice of gospel and civil rights / Barbara Kramer.
    p. cm. — (African-American biographies)
  Summary: A biography of the renowned gospel singer who hoped that
her art would further the cause of civil rights for African Americans.
Includes bibliographical references (p.   ) and index.
  Discography: p.
  ISBN 0-7660-2115-7 (hardcover)
    1. Jackson, Mahalia, 1911–1972—Juvenile literature. 2. Gospel
musicians—United States—Biography—Juvenile literature. [1. Jackson,
Mahalia, 1911–1972. 2. Singers. 3. African Americans—Biography.
4. Women—Biography.] I. Title. II. Series.
ML3930.J2 K7 2003
782.25'4'092—dc21

                                                        2002014310

To Our Readers:
We have done our best to make sure all Internet Addresses in this book were
active and appropriate when we went to press. However, the author and the
publisher have no control over and assume no liability for the material available
on those Internet sites or on other Web sites they may link to. Any comments or
suggestions can be sent by e-mail to comments@enslow.com or to the address on
the back cover.

Every effort has been made to locate all copyright holders of material used in this
book. If any errors or omissions have occurred, corrections will be made in future
editions of this book.

CONTENTS

Mahalia Jackson

1

"I Been 'Buked And I Been Scorned"

It was August 28, 1963, a day that would go down in history. That afternoon, at the March on Washington for Jobs and Freedom, Dr. Martin Luther King, Jr., would deliver his famous "I Have a Dream" speech. Important civil rights legislation would later pass as a result of this major civil rights demonstration in Washington, D.C.

Another unforgettable voice would echo through the crowds on this momentous day. Mahalia Jackson had come to the nation's capital to sing. When Dr. King invited her to perform, he even suggested a song for her to sing. It was an old spiritual, "I Been 'Buked and I Been Scorned."

Organizers of the march had been busy planning for months. On June 19, 1963, President John F. Kennedy had sent his proposed civil rights bill to Congress. The bill would give African Americans many rights long denied to them because of racial segregation and discrimination. In some states in the Deep South, African Americans were not allowed to vote. They could not attend schools or use parks or other public facilities designated for whites only. Southern restaurants, theaters, and other businesses were also segregated, keeping blacks and whites separate in almost all aspects of their lives. Even drinking fountains were labeled for blacks or whites only.

The proposed civil rights bill would grant African Americans the right to vote and to use public facilities without discrimination. Some people did not think that was enough. They wanted an expanded bill that would also protect African Americans from being treated unfairly in the workplace. Organizers of the march urged people to come to Washington, D.C., to show their support for a stronger civil rights bill.

On the morning of August 28, 1963, the sun rose in a clear blue sky, but there were not many marchers in sight. By 7:00 A.M., only a few thousand people milled about on the grassy area near the Washington Monument, where everyone was to gather. But throughout the morning, that number quickly grew as people arrived on buses they had chartered for the event. According to a report in *The New York Times*, more than fifteen hundred buses and twenty-one special trains brought people from all across the United States. Eighty-seven people from Los Angeles had chartered a plane. Others came by car or van, and a group from Brooklyn, New York, made the 237-mile trip on foot.

Before the day was over, more than two hundred thousand people would gather. About sixty thousand of them were white. At 11:30 A.M., the marchers began their almost one mile walk down Constitution and Independence avenues to the Lincoln Memorial.

While they marched, Mahalia Jackson found a seat on the platform set up at the Lincoln Memorial for special guests. Singers Lena Horne and Sammy Davis, Jr., and author James Baldwin sat nearby. Other familiar faces on the platform included actors Paul Newman, James Garner, and Sydney Poitier. Jackson watched as the marchers paraded along both sides of the Reflecting Pool. Some sang songs such as "We Shall Overcome," the unofficial anthem of the civil rights movement. Others chanted phrases such as, "FREEDOM—FREEDOM—FREEDOM!"[1]

The demonstrators sat on either side of the Reflecting Pool and in the grassy areas surrounding the monument, ready for an afternoon of music,

Jackson's singing was one of the highlights of the March on Washington. Among those on the speakers' stage were Martin Luther King, Jr., bottom right, and his wife, Coretta Scott King (in sunglasses, seated behind the microphones).

speeches, and prayer. Forty television cameras had been set up at the Lincoln Memorial, providing live coverage of the event to millions of at-home viewers.

Jackson was scheduled to sing near the end of the program after a long list of speakers. By the time her turn came, people were hot, tired, and restless. Many had already left and others were starting to leave, but they stopped when Jackson stepped up to the microphone. She sang without accompaniment, beginning slowly, softly. "I been 'buked and I been scorned / I'm gonna tell my Lord / When I get home / Just how long you've been treating me wrong."[2]

When murmurs from the crowd indicated that she had their attention, she began to pick up the beat. She clapped her hands, swayed, and sang louder. Her clear, strong voice "seemed to bounce off the Capitol far up the mall," one reporter noted.[3]

Then, in the midst of her song, an airplane buzzed overhead, creating a distraction. Author Studs Terkel described what happened next: "She just looked up at the plane, but she *sang* up to the plane. And, so help me, her voice drowned out the buzz!"[4] Thousands of people around the Reflecting Pool waved white handkerchiefs in tribute. When her song ended, they stood and cheered.

Jackson's performance brought tears to many eyes. A *New York Times* reporter called it one of two "emotional high points of the day."[5] The other high point, which came shortly after Jackson's song, was Dr. King's memorable "I Have a Dream" speech.

Being part of that program was a special triumph for Jackson, who had experienced her share of racial prejudice over the years. But through her music, she had won the love and respect of people of all races all around the world. That was something that she could never have imagined as a child growing up in poverty in New Orleans, Louisiana.

2

A Small Girl With a Big Voice

ahalia Jackson was named Mahala after one of her mother's sisters, Mahala Paul. Mahalia later added an "i" to her name, but her family and friends just called her Halie.

There is some confusion about her birth date. Records at City Hall in New Orleans state that she was born in 1911. But Mahalia's aunts disagreed. Mahalia was born a few months after her cousin Porterfield. He was born in 1912, so Mahalia could not have been born in 1911. October 26, 1912, was the correct date, the aunts said.

Mahalia was born in this house in New Orleans.

Mahalia's mother, Charity Clark, already had a three-year-old son, Peter Roosevelt Hunter. Mahalia, her brother, and her mother lived with some of Charity Clark's six sisters and four of Mahalia's cousins. At one point, thirteen people all lived together in the small home.

Charity Clark could not afford to take time off from work, so she returned to her job as a domestic for a white family soon after Mahalia's birth. That left Aunt Bell, her cousin Porterfield's mother, to nurse both babies—Porterfield and Mahalia. The other aunts also helped with the babies.

Mahalia was born with an eye infection, so her aunts kept her in a darkened room. They were concerned that any light would cause her to go blind. They washed her eyes often until the infection cleared. Mahalia also had bowed legs. Her aunts treated that problem with leg massages. But it was not until later, after years of healthy eating, that her legs finally straightened.

Mahalia's father, Johnny Jackson, lived nearby in a house he shared with his parents. During the day, he worked on the docks as a stevedore, loading cotton onto ships on the Mississippi River. He earned extra money working as a barber in the evenings. On Sundays, he preached at the Plymouth Rock Baptist Church.

Johnny Jackson did not show much interest in Mahalia, but his parents always welcomed her. Mahalia visited them whenever she got a chance. All of Mahalia's grandparents had been born slaves. Mahalia liked to hear her grandfather Jackson tell about his first taste of freedom after the Civil War. He had walked off the plantation and kept on walking until he arrived in New Orleans, almost one hundred miles away.

Mahalia began singing at an early age. "From what my folks told me I guess I was singing almost as soon as I was out of the cradle," she said later. "I always had a big voice and I loved to use it."[1] When she was four years old, she sang in the children's choir at church.

Mahalia was only five years old when her mother died. The cause of her death at the age of thirty is not known. The family took Charity Clark's body back to the plantation where she had been born. Charity Clark's father, Paul Clark, was a minister who still lived on the plantation. He buried his daughter in a small cemetery next to the church where he preached.

After the funeral, there was a discussion among Mahalia's aunts about where Mahalia and her brother would live. Having Mahalia move in with her father was not a possibility. By that time, Johnny Jackson had married and moved into his own home. He and his wife had two children. Mahalia could visit him at the barbershop where he worked, but she was not welcome in their home. Aunt Mahala Paul ended the discussion when she announced that she would take both Mahalia and Peter.

Mahala Paul, known to most people as Aunt Duke, worked as a cook for a wealthy white family. She was married to Emanuel Paul, a bricklayer and plasterer. Their son, Fred, was several years older than Mahalia.

Mahalia and Peter moved in with the Pauls, about six blocks from the house where Mahalia was born. "We lived in a little old shack where the railroad ran so close it shook the bedrooms," Jackson recalled.[2] Beyond the tracks was the levee, a high grassy riverbank built up to hold back the floodwaters of the Mississippi.

The house was clean, but it needed repairs. "You could be in the house and you could see the sun outside, through the roof," Jackson said. "If it rained, it rained inside. We'd rush about putting pots and pans around the floor to catch the run-off before we got flooded."[3]

There were no toys in the house. Mahalia made her own rag doll, braiding grass to use as hair. But there was little time for play. While Aunt Duke was at work, Mahalia had chores to do at home. She dusted the furniture and scrubbed the floors with lye, a strong chemical.

As Mahalia grew, the list of chores got longer. She learned to iron as soon as she was tall enough to see over the ironing board. She gathered driftwood along the Mississippi River and spread it out in the sun to dry. They used the driftwood for cooking and heating. She also picked up coal along the railroad tracks to be used for heating. She made mattresses from cotton cement sacks and stuffed them with corn husks and the Spanish moss that hung from the trees. She learned to weave chair seats from sugarcane stalks and palms.

If the work was not done just right, Aunt Duke punished Mahalia with the cat-o'-nine-tails. That strap got its name from the nine cords, or tails, that were attached to the handle.

Although Aunt Duke was stern, Emanuel Paul was kind and gentle. Mahalia liked helping him in the garden. The family was poor, but they always had food.

Much of it came from their large garden, where they grew green beans, red beans, peas, tomatoes, pumpkins, corn, okra, and mustard greens.

The family also raised chickens and goats. They caught fish, shrimp, crabs, and turtles in the river. Sometimes for breakfast they ate baby alligator, which Mahalia helped catch. She learned to sneak up on the young alligators while they sunned themselves on the riverbank. Then she would smack them on the head with a stick before they had a chance to slip away.

Many of the men in Mahalia's neighborhood, including her father and cousin Fred, worked on the docks loading cotton onto ships.

Aunt Duke smothered the alligator tails with onions and garlic and baked them in the oven. In the woods, the family hunted raccoon, rabbit, and possum, and they picked bananas, figs, oranges, and pecan nuts from the trees.

Mahalia's neighborhood was home to a mixture of Italians, French, and African Americans. There were also Creoles, whose ancestors were a combination of Europeans and African Americans. Those different ethnic groups lived side by side, and the children all played together. But outside the neighborhood were signs that read WHITES ONLY or COLORED.

Segregation was allowed then, the result of the U.S. Supreme Court's *Plessy* v. *Ferguson* ruling in 1896. The Court said that segregation was legal as long as there were equal facilities for blacks. Although the facilities for blacks were not at all equal to what was available to whites, many states, including Louisiana, still practiced segregation. That meant that Mahalia was not allowed to go to the school where white children in her neighborhood went. Instead, Mahalia attended a nearby school for black children. McDonough School Number 24 was a wooden building divided into two halves by a long hallway. Boys had classes on one side of the building, and girls on the other.

When Mahalia was seven, Charity Clark's youngest sister came to live at the Pauls' home. Aunt Bessie, who was twelve, already had a job working for a white family.

Mahalia went to work with her. They started early in the morning, getting the children ready for school and doing dishes. After school, they went back and worked some more, earning $2 a week for their time.

Mahalia did not mind the work, and the family was kind to her. They gave her hand-me-down clothes and they believed in a custom in New Orleans known as "the pan." It meant that Mahalia and Bessie were allowed to take home leftover food.

For recreation, Mahalia went to the Mount Moriah Baptist Church. At the back of the church was the Community House where children gathered to sing and play games. On Saturday nights, silent movies were shown. The admission price of five or ten cents was cheaper than going downtown to a movie theater.

Mahalia sang in the church choir, but she liked singing with the congregation better. "All around me I could hear a real jubilant expression, the feet tapping and the hands clapping," she later recalled. "Even today I feel that same bounce when I sing."[4]

Mahalia also enjoyed spending time on the levee with her friends. They lit a campfire, then gathered around it to talk, sing, and eat pecans and sugarcane. Sometimes they roasted sweet potatoes in the embers of the campfire.

Music was an important part of Mahalia's childhood. "I remember singing as I scrubbed floors. It would make the work go easier," she said later.[5] She listened to the work songs of the men on the docks. In the evenings, she could hear the music of small bands performing on the showboats on the Mississippi River.

Mahalia also listened to the singing of the Pentecostal Church near the Pauls' home. The congregation sang to the accompaniment of tambourines, drums, and cymbals. "Everybody sang and clapped and stomped their feet, sang with their whole bodies!" Jackson later said.[6] Aunt Duke would not let Mahalia go into the church, but she could sit outside on the steps of their home and listen.

Aunt Duke believed that music other than what was sung in church was the devil's music. She allowed only church music in her home, but she could not control her son, Fred. Mahalia's cousin Fred worked on the docks and was also a part-time musician, playing the guitar. "He got along with the gambling men and music men and he knew the sporting life downtown," Jackson recalled. "He loved music and he bought all the blues and jazz records he could."[7]

When Aunt Duke was away at her job, Mahalia listened to Fred's records while she worked. Her favorite was blues singer Bessie Smith, although she could not say exactly why. "All I know is it would grip me. Bessie's singing gave me the same feeling as when I'd hear men singing outside as they worked, laying the ties for the railroad, working on the docks,"

Jackson said.[8] Mahalia sang along with Smith's records, imitating her style.

Jazz bands played on the backs of trucks as they rode around town advertising their upcoming performances. Lesser-known bands played at lawn parties. "New Orleans was noted for its beautiful lawn parties," Jackson recalled.[9] Yards were decorated with Chinese lanterns, and sawdust was strewn on the grass to make it easier for people to dance.

New Orleans was also known for its unique style of funerals. Family members or friends hired brass bands to play at funerals for important people, usually men. The coffin was placed in a wagon drawn by two or four white horses. The band followed behind the wagon on the way to the cemetery, playing slow songs such as "Nearer My God to Thee" and "What a Friend We Have in Jesus."

On the way back from the cemetery, the band played livelier songs such as "When the Saints Go Marching In." Men, women, and children danced and followed along behind the band. This was known as the Second Line. They danced in celebration of life, even though it was a sad occasion.

One New Orleans tradition that Mahalia did not like was Mardi Gras, the colorful festivities held every year several weeks before Easter. The Mardi Gras celebration in Mahalia's part of town was very different from the one downtown. "The white people would

Mardi Gras was celebrated with great fanfare in downtown New Orleans, above. But in Mahalia's neighborhood, it was a frightful occasion for fighting and crime.

have theirs with the big floats down the main part of Canal Street, which were very beautiful and high class," she recalled.[10] But in her neighborhood, people from different gangs used that occasion to settle old arguments. Often people were killed in fights during Mardi Gras. With their faces hidden behind masks, gang members felt freer to commit crimes.

Mahalia's formal education ended in grade school. In some interviews, she said that she had to leave school and go to work after the eighth grade. Other times, she said that she quit school when she was only ten years old. Later in life, she was embarrassed about her lack of education and was not entirely honest about the amount of schooling she had. "It gave me a sort of complex," she once said.[11]

She was also disappointed. She wanted to be a nurse, and for that she needed an education. Instead, she had to quit school and get a job to contribute to the family income. She baby-sat and did laundry. She was a good, fast laundress. She could iron a man's shirt in only three minutes. But she wanted something more.

Many of the people Mahalia knew left New Orleans looking for a better life in the North. Chicago was a popular destination. Two of Mahalia's aunts moved to Chicago. Her uncle Emanuel worked as a bricklayer there for a while, sending his earnings home to the family. Mahalia's cousin Fred had also left New Orleans. He got a job playing with a band from Kansas City.

Lying in bed at night, Mahalia dreamed of her future. "Someday the sun is going to shine on me in some faraway place," she vowed.[12]

3

A NEW START

Hearing Aunt Duke's cries, Mahalia came running in to see what was wrong. Near her aunt lay a telegram with terrible news. Aunt Duke's son—Mahalia's cousin Fred—was dead.

Mahalia never found out how Fred had died. Some people said that he had been killed in an after-hours barroom fight. His body was sent back to New Orleans, where Fred's musician friends honored him with a brass band for the funeral. Mahalia had been too young to understand her mother's death, but now, at age fourteen, she felt great sadness at Fred's funeral.[1] She took his death as a sign that it was time for her to leave New Orleans. Fred had always encouraged her to get out and do something with her singing talent.

Adding to Mahalia's unhappiness were her arguments with Aunt Duke, who expected Mahalia to follow her strict rules. One particular quarrel with Aunt Duke made Mahalia even more determined to find a new life elsewhere.

It began after Mahalia was late getting home one evening. She and her cousin Celie had stopped at a friend's house, where there was a party. Mahalia saw Celie talking to a young man near the punch bowl. Later, Mahalia noticed that Celie was trying to fight off the young man's advances. Mahalia grabbed the closest thing at hand, an ice pick, and stabbed the young man with it. It barely punctured his skin, but it was enough to get his attention and get him away from Celie.

Mahalia's friends urged her to hurry home and let them take care of the young man. They knew that Mahalia was not allowed to stay out past nine o'clock, and they did not want her to get into trouble. But she had already stayed out too long, and Aunt Duke was angry when she found out what had happened. She told Mahalia to get out of the house and not come back. Mahalia spent the night with friends.

It was not the first time Aunt Duke had ordered Mahalia to leave. Other times, Mahalia stayed away for a night or two and then went back home after Aunt Duke had calmed down. But this time Mahalia did not return.

She moved into a tiny house that had only one room and a kitchen. It was just a couple of blocks away from Aunt Duke's. Friends and family helped out by giving her furniture they no longer needed, and Mahalia looked for more work so that she could pay the rent, $6 a month. At fifteen, Mahalia was on her own.

Life changed for Mahalia again later that year when her aunt Hannah came down from Chicago for Thanksgiving. Aunt Hannah invited Mahalia back to Chicago. Aunt Duke did not want Mahalia to go. She warned Mahalia that Chicago was home to dangerous gangsters like Al Capone and "Bugsy" Malone.

Mahalia's father rarely got involved in her life, but on this matter he sided with Aunt Duke. He had been to Chicago once. He returned home frightened by the size of the city and the presence of gangsters. Their warnings worried Mahalia, but she decided to go anyway.

She used some of her savings to buy a train ticket to Chicago. In 1927, all African Americans had to ride in a segregated train car—the first car behind the engine. They were not allowed to eat in the dining car, so Aunt Hannah packed a large basket of food to take along. Their only chance to get anything hot was at stations along the way. When the trains stopped, they could lean out a window and buy coffee from peddlers on the platform.

The trip took two nights and a day, but Mahalia and her aunt had nowhere to lie down. While white passengers rested comfortably in Pullman berths, Mahalia and Aunt Hannah had to sit upright in their seats. They huddled together under a wool blanket that Aunt Hannah had brought along for the unheated segregated car.

It was cold and snowy when they arrived in Chicago. Mahalia did not have any clothing warm enough for such temperatures, and she expected a cold walk to Aunt Hannah's place. She was surprised when her aunt hailed a taxi and the white driver did not protest.[2] In New Orleans, they would never have been allowed to ride in a white man's cab.

Aunt Hannah lived in a three-story building on Chicago's South Side. She shared the apartment with her sister Alice. Mahalia moved in with her two aunts and her young cousins Nathaniel and Little Alice.

What did Mahalia think about this new city? "At first I was afraid of Chicago," she later recalled. "I couldn't get used to the noise and the cold and those big buildings that made me feel like I was in a prison."[3]

But she also saw something she liked: African Americans in Chicago were prospering. The city had a large African-American community, second in size only to New York City's Harlem. More than three hundred thousand African Americans lived in the city's South Side neighborhood, in an area covering almost forty blocks. There was work in Chicago. Many from the

South Side found jobs in Chicago's meatpacking industry or in the steel mills in nearby Gary, Indiana.

Mahalia was amazed to see African-American policemen, firemen, and professionals. It was so different from her neighborhood in New Orleans, where all the policemen were white and she had never seen an African-American lawyer. In Chicago, African-American doctors worked at the Provident Hospital, where Mahalia hoped to train as a nurse. Blacks owned their own businesses, and they even had their own weekly newspaper, *The Chicago Defender*. "It gave me inspiration to see these things," Jackson said. "I thought about someday having a business of my own."[4]

Mahalia had to put her nursing plans on hold when Aunt Hannah became sick with heart trouble. Mahalia filled in at her aunt's job as a cook for a white family. Aunt Alice was also a cook. Six days a week, Mahalia and Aunt Alice boarded the elevated train known as the El. That system of railroad tracks built above the city's streets took them to their jobs across town on the North Side. When Aunt Hannah was well enough to go back to work, the family asked Mahalia to continue working for them doing laundry.

Soon after she arrived in Chicago, Mahalia heard that Bessie Smith would be appearing at the Avenue Theater. Mahalia went early and waited in line to be sure she got a ticket. It was worth the wait. "She filled the whole place with her voice," Jackson later recalled.⁵ Mahalia sat in her seat long after everyone else had left the concert, just thinking about Smith's performance. She did not leave until the ushers told her that they were ready to lock up for the night.

At Mahalia's first visit to a Chicago church, she discovered that services there were different. In New Orleans, she was used to singing with the congregation. Mahalia did not know that in the Chicago church, the choir sang the hymns and the congregation listened. When the choir began to sing, Mahalia felt moved to join in. As people turned to stare, Mahalia realized that hers was the only voice coming from the back of the church. Still, she did not stop. "I kept on singing, and people looking at me, and I just held my head up and my eyes closed. And finally somebody else would pick it up and finally another person would pick it up until the whole church joined in," she recalled.⁶

Mahalia realized the irony of the situation. She knew that many of the people in that church had come to Chicago from the South. Like her, they were used to singing with the congregation. But they had abandoned that practice up north as if it were too undignified.

Mahalia soon joined the Greater Salem Baptist Church, where she hoped to sing with the choir. There were fifty people in the choir, and at Mahalia's first practice she sang louder than all of them together. When the choir director stopped them midsong,

Mahalia was sure that she was going to be asked to leave. Instead, he asked her to try a solo. Mahalia picked "Hand Me Down My Silver Trumpet, Gabriel," a song she had known since she was a child. But now she was so nervous that she prayed that she would be able to make it all the way through to the end. She did not need to worry. The director made her a soloist with the choir.

Mahalia also became friends with the minister's three sons—Prince, Robert, and Wilbur Johnson—and a woman named Louise Lemon. By 1929, the Johnson brothers teamed up with Louise Lemon and Mahalia to form a group called the Johnson Gospel Singers.

At first, they sang only in their own church, but they soon began getting invitations from other churches in the area. Their style included handclapping and songs with a bouncy beat. Many people enjoyed their music, but there were some who said that it did not belong in church. "Get that twisting and that jazz out of his church," one pastor hollered.[7]

Mahalia did not leave quietly. "This is the way we sing down South!" she called over her shoulder as she headed out the door.[8]

In 1929, the stock market crashed. This marked the beginning of the Great Depression, an economic crisis that affected the whole country. People lost their jobs when businesses shut down and factories laid off employees. People lost their savings when banks were forced to close.

Jackson saw the effects of the Great Depression in her neighborhood. Unemployment was especially high among African Americans on the South Side of Chicago. They had been the last to be hired at factories as they migrated north, and now they were the first to lose their jobs. All the new prosperity they had enjoyed was gone. "It was as if somebody had pulled a switch and everything had stopped running," Jackson recalled.[9]

With no jobs to go to, people roamed the streets aimlessly. Families moved in together, hoping that between them they would be able to come up with enough money to pay the rent. Those without money for rent lived in shacks pieced together from scraps of wood, tin, and tarpaper. Soup kitchens and breadlines were set up to provide food for those who were down on their luck.

In an odd twist of fate, the Depression actually helped Jackson's singing career.

One way that people paid their bills during those hard times was with rent parties, which included supper and music at a private home. Admission to the parties raised money to help keep a roof over the homeowner's head. They also helped musicians make a living by giving them a place to perform.

The Great Depression hit hard in Chicago neighborhoods like this one. "It was as if somebody had pulled a switch and everything had stopped running," said Jackson.

Churches were doing the same type of thing, only they called the parties "socials." The Johnson Gospel Singers performed often at socials in Chicago churches. For an evening's performance, they averaged about $1.50 each from a collection taken or from an admission charge of five or ten cents.

The Johnson Gospel Singers' reputation grew. They soon began receiving invitations to appear in churches in other parts of Illinois and in Indiana. Jackson also started getting opportunities as a soloist.

In 1931, the owner of a local funeral home hired Jackson to sing at funerals, paying her $2 for each service. He also booked other performances for her in Chicago and the surrounding area. To advertise her concerts, he printed flyers on his copy machine and used the funeral car to drive her to singing engagements.

Jackson also sang for local politicians. In the summer of 1932, William L. Dawson was running for a seat on the city council. He asked Jackson to perform at his fund-raising functions. Jackson had a special interest in helping him get elected. He was African American and understood the problems in her neighborhood.

She kept busy that summer singing for large meetings and political rallies. She sang her gospel music, but changed the words of the songs to fit the occasion. At political rallies, Jackson sang about how well Dawson would serve his people. Dawson won that election. He later went on to serve fourteen terms as a Democratic congressman in the U.S. House of Representatives.

Jackson also teamed up with musician Thomas A. Dorsey. Using the stage name Georgia Tom, Dorsey had traveled and performed with blues singer Ma Rainey. Although he had a successful blues career, he was the son of a Baptist minister and had been raised to believe that the blues was the devil's music. In 1930, he gave up the blues and turned his attention to writing gospel music.

In 1932, Dorsey opened the first publishing house for sheet music of gospel songs written by African-American composers. At first, not many people bought his sheet music. Then he got the idea of using demonstrators. These were performers who stood on street corners and sang the music. People heard the songs, and they liked them. They were then more willing to pay a dime for a copy of the sheet music. Jackson became one of Dorsey's demonstrators.

Dorsey had first heard Jackson when she was singing with the Johnson Gospel Singers, and he was impressed. "[They] were really rocking them everywhere they went," Dorsey recalled.[10]

He also liked the way Mahalia worked a crowd. "She was a good mixer . . . and she loved everybody," he said. "At least she acted like she loved everybody. She called everybody 'baby, honey, darling.'"[11]

On the other hand, Dorsey thought that there were areas where Mahalia could improve. He said that she did not breathe in the right places, and that she sang songs too fast. "I tried to show Mahalia how to breathe and phrase, but she wouldn't listen. She said I was trying to make a stereotyped singer out of her," Dorsey explained. "She may have been right."[12]

Dorsey would not be the only one to try to change Jackson's style. Jackson had no musical training. In fact, she could not even read music. With new opportunities coming her way, she decided that maybe it was time for her to get some formal training. In 1932, she signed up for a lesson with an African-American tenor who had a studio on Chicago's South Side.

Lessons cost $4 an hour, which was a lot of money at that time. At her first lesson, the instructor told Jackson that she needed to sing slower and to stop hollering so that white people could understand her music. It was confusing to Jackson, who felt that he was asking her to sing in a way that was not natural to her.[13] She never went back for another lesson.

Jackson continued doing laundry during the day. That income and the money from singing with the Johnson Gospel Singers and as a soloist did not add up to much. But she knew that she was better off than so many others who were out of work during the Great Depression.

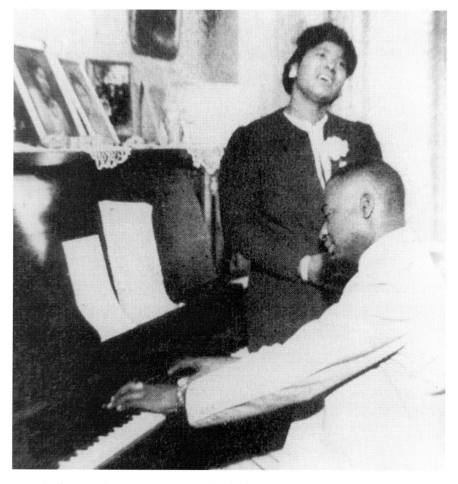

Jackson rehearses a song with Thomas A. Dorsey. Her street performances inspired many people to buy copies of his sheet music.

One day, on her way home from work, Jackson saw a group of people standing in a soup line. It did not seem right to her that they were waiting in line for soup when she had money in her pocket. She decided to take action. "I just told a bunch of those guys to come on over to my house and I cooked string beans, and ham hocks, and cornbread, and neck bones, and rice. I must have fed about twenty people," she recalled.[14] After that, she made it a habit. If she saw people standing in a soup line and she had the money to give them some good home-cooked food, she invited them home with her.

Jackson was busy performing both as a soloist and as part of the Johnson Gospel Singers. But there was always the question of whether or not it was possible to make a living as a gospel singer. Jackson did not have the answer, but she knew that she wanted to continue singing. Other members of the Johnson Gospel Singers were not as committed. As they turned to other interests, Jackson began performing more often as a soloist.

4

A "FISH-AND-BREAD" SINGER

By the mid-1930s, Jackson was touring all across the United States. She traveled by train and sang at churches affiliated with the National Baptist Convention, an organization of more than 4 million people. She went from one church to another, staying with the minister's family in each town. After a concert, they would count up the money. Then the minister would subtract for Jackson's room and board, and they would divide up the rest. Often, performers such as Jackson were invited to stay and eat supper with the church members after a concert. That was how they became known as "fish-and-bread"

singers. They sang for the Lord and also for their supper.

Jackson sang traditional gospel songs, but not in a traditional way. Her style was a combination of blues, the Baptist music she sang as a child, and the rhythms of the Pentecostal Church near her childhood home in New Orleans. She sang with her whole body, strutting and swinging her hips. She believed that gospel music should be sung with joy. For those who thought that her handclapping and foot stomping did not belong in church, she had a ready answer. "Oh clap your hands, all ye people; shout unto the Lord with the voice of a trumpet," she said, quoting from Psalm 47 in the Bible.[1]

Jackson's powerful voice was an asset in those early travels. "There were no mikes in churches in those days," Jackson recalled. "I just sang out, and with the Lord's help the people in the back rows heard me."[2]

Jackson continued doing laundry in Chicago between singing engagements. Then, after being gone on a long tour, she came back to find that she had been replaced. She got a job packing dates in a factory, but it did not take her long to discover that she was not suited to that work. "After a week in that factory I was ready to have them put me in a box!" she joked.[3] She then got a job as a maid in a hotel, earning $12 a week.

Jackson was singing at a church social in 1935 when she met Isaac "Ike" Hockenhull. Jackson was twenty-three, and Hockenhull was ten years older. He was well

By the mid-1930s, Jackson's gospel singing was energizing worshipers in Baptist churches all across the United States.

educated, with a degree in chemistry from Fisk University in Tennessee. He had also studied at Tuskegee University in Alabama. Hockenhull was immediately drawn to her.

Jackson found it hard to believe that an older, educated man could be interested in her, but Hockenhull was captivated. "I loved her the minute I laid eyes on her across that room," he said. "We talked, that evening, and then I called on her and Hannah and Alice."[4] They dated for about a year. In 1936, they married in a small ceremony in Aunt Hannah's apartment.

Some time earlier, Jackson had taken a ten-year-old homeless boy named John Sellers under her wing. He lived with Hockenhull and Jackson for a short time, and Hockenhull proved to be a good father. When Jackson discovered that the youngster had a great singing voice, she began letting him perform at some of her concerts. She introduced him as Little Brother John Sellers.

During the Depression, Hockenhull could not find work as a chemist. Instead, he worked as a substitute mail carrier for the postal service. His mother had run a cosmetics business in St. Louis before the Depression. She specialized in cosmetics and hair products designed for African-American women. Hockenhull knew the formulas she used, and he and Jackson began mixing up their own products to sell from their home. Jackson took the products on the road with her to sell. Hockenhull also sold them in Chicago to people along his mail route.

In 1937, J. Mayo "Ink" Williams of Decca Records contacted Jackson about making a recording. At that time, Decca was the third-largest record company in the United States, but Jackson would be its first gospel singer. A recording session was set for May 21, 1937.

The 78-rpm records of the time were able to hold only three or three and a half minutes of music on each side, one song per side. Traditionally, record producers picked one song that they believed would do well, and that became the hit side of the record. A weaker song was placed on the back, or flip, side. It was also customary to record songs for more than one record during a recording session.

Jackson recorded four songs during her first session, including "God's Goin' to Separate the Wheat from the Tares." The song was about getting rid of the weeds (tares) before the wheat could be harvested. The song enjoyed some success in the South, but did not get much playing time elsewhere.

Another song from that recording session, "God Shall Wipe Away All My Tears," was a big hit in Jackson's old neighborhood in New Orleans. The men who supplied records for jukeboxes in barrooms discovered that Jackson had been raised in that area. So they installed the record on local jukeboxes. It was the first time that a gospel record had received that kind of attention. Jackson's family never went to barrooms. But when they heard that she was on the jukebox, they made an exception. Even Aunt Duke went down to listen to her niece on the jukebox.

Unfortunately, overall sales of Jackson's records were low. Decca executives wanted her to sing blues, but Jackson said no. It was not that she did not like the blues. She said that it was beautiful music, but it did not leave her feeling satisfied. "It's like a man that drinks, and when he gets through being drunk he's still got his trouble," she explained.[5] When she refused to sing blues, Decca dropped her from its list of artists.

Other people also told Jackson that she should sing other types of music. One was Jackson's friend Louis "Satchmo" Armstrong, who had found worldwide fame as a jazz musician. He wowed audiences with his trumpet playing and his distinctive gravelly voice. He tried to persuade Jackson to sing with his band, telling her that she could make "some real green," but she said no.[6]

Jackson's husband, Ike, also wanted her to sing something other than gospel. He urged her to train in classical music such as opera. "He thought gospel singing wasn't educated," Jackson explained.[7]

Disagreements about Jackson's music were just one of the problems in their marriage. Hockenhull also did not like Jackson's being on the road so much. By the late 1930s, she was traveling with Thomas A. Dorsey, singing his songs in churches and at Baptist conventions all across the country.

Jackson was unhappy with Hockenhull because he spent his time betting on racehorses. "I was brought up in the church and I did not want that gambling money," she said.[8] Gambling losses also put a strain on their finances. The situation got even worse when Hockenhull was laid off from the post office. Jackson had also lost her job. She was fired from the hotel after a glitch in train connections caused her to miss work one Monday.

They were down to their last few dollars when Hockenhull heard about casting for a Federal Theater Project in Chicago. The Federal Theater Project was part of a government agency formed during the Depression to provide work for unemployed writers, stagehands, musicians, and others involved with the stage. Now the project was casting for a swing production of Gilbert and Sullivan's operetta *The Mikado*. Swing was a new type of jazz with smoother, less complicated rhythms. It was often played by large dance bands. The new production, called *The Hot Mikado*, would feature an all-black cast.

Jackson did not want to audition, but Hockenhull said they needed the money. She took her gospel songbook and headed for the theater. She was greeted at the door by a young woman who informed her that the songbook would not do. She needed sheet music. Jackson went to a nearby store and spent fifty cents for an arrangement of "Sometimes I Feel Like a Motherless Child," a song that was already in her book of gospel music.

When it was her turn to audition, Jackson gave the music to the pianist, who began to play. It was not an arrangement that Jackson knew. Since she did not read music, she did not know when to start singing. The pianist stopped and started again. This time Jackson came in at the right time.

Jackson sang from the heart, but she did not get any pleasure from knowing that she had done well. "I was chancing my soul for a dollar, and it was just like hot grease popping at me to hear the people in that auditorium applaud," she remembered.[9]

When she got home, Hockenhull met her at the door to tell her that the theater had already called. Jackson got the part. Then she learned that her husband had also had some success that day. He had gotten a job selling insurance. That settled it. With Hockenhull working, they no longer needed the extra money. To Hockenhull's disappointment, Jackson called the theater and told them that she would not take the part.

In 1939, Jackson decided to pursue another dream—having her own business. She opened Mahalia's Beauty Salon, which was an immediate success. She soon had five women working for her. An added benefit was that there was room for Jackson and Hockenhull to live at the back of the shop so they did not have to pay rent for an apartment.

Jackson continued to travel on weekends for singing engagements, arriving home in time to open her beauty salon on Mondays. In spite of her hard work, she and her husband struggled financially because of Hockenhull's gambling.

Hockenhull sometimes won at the racetrack, but he was not good at managing money. One time, after a big win at the track, he gave Jackson $2,000 and told her to hide it so that he would not be tempted to use it. Jackson stowed the money under the carpet in the bedroom, spreading it out smoothly so that there were no noticeable lumps. Then she left for a tour. When Jackson came back, the money was gone. Hockenhull had used it to buy a racehorse.

A final blow to their marriage started as a happy occasion when Hockenhull bought Jackson her first car, a new white Buick. Having a car made traveling easier for Jackson. She was no longer dependent on train schedules. Often Hockenhull or a friend or relative traveled with her to do the driving.

One day, Jackson looked out the window of her beauty salon to see men hooking up her car to a tow truck. They were repossessing it because Hockenhull had not been making the car payments. Jackson paid the

Jackson's first car was a gift from her husband.

money owed, and she was able to keep the car. But she was tired of paying Hockenhull's gambling debts. The couple separated in 1941 and got a divorce in 1943.

By the end of 1941, the United States was fighting in World War II. The war caused shortages of products such as gasoline, which made traveling more difficult. Jackson gave up touring with Dorsey and accepted a position as choir director at a Chicago church. She was also still busy with her beauty salon.

In the early 1940s, the popularity of gospel music grew as people sought comfort in the face of the tragedies of war. When the war ended in 1945, a new group of concert promoters sprang up to take advantage of that growing interest. The promoters organized concerts for gospel singers. Then the promoters and performers each got a share of the money taken in at the door.

Sadly, some of the new promoters were not honest. They reported earnings lower than what was actually made in ticket sales. That meant less money for the performers. Jackson vowed that she would not be a victim of dishonest promoters. She liked to place someone she trusted at the door selling tickets. That way she could be certain about how much money was taken in. Sometimes she even sold the tickets herself.

Some people thought it was strange to have the performer selling tickets for her own concert. One time before a concert at a church in Chicago, Jackson and two assistants sat in the box office selling tickets. A press agent half jokingly told Jackson that he was going to have a photographer take a picture of the show's star sitting in the ticket booth. His intention was to embarrass Jackson enough to leave the box office, but she was not budging. "That'll show some of those dishonest promoters I got sense enough to protect my money," she said.[10]

There were also promoters who left before the concert was over without paying the performers. As a result, Jackson refused to sing until she had received full payment. She also insisted on being paid in cash and was known to carry large amounts of money in her purse or tucked into her clothing for safekeeping.

Jackson had just finished performing at a gospel concert in Detroit, Michigan, in 1946, when a man came up to introduce himself. He was Johnny Meyers, a well-known black gospel promoter in New York City. That meeting steered Jackson's career in a new direction.

5

"MOVE ON UP
A LITTLE HIGHER"

ohnny Meyers rented large auditoriums for gospel concerts. They had more seats than the churches where Jackson usually sang. One place Meyers liked in particular was the Golden Gate Ballroom in New York City. He offered Jackson $1,000 to sing there in September 1946. On the night of the concert, Bess Berman, president and owner of Apollo Records, was in the audience. Not long after the show, she talked to Jackson about recording for Apollo.

Jackson's first recording session for Apollo Records was on October 3, 1946. She worked with Art Freeman, music director and arranger for Apollo, to record four songs, enough for two 78-rpm records. Unfortunately, neither record sold well, and Berman told Freeman to let Jackson go. Even Jackson had decided that the recording industry was not yet ready for gospel music. But Freeman had one more idea he wanted to try. He thought Jackson should record "Move On Up a Little Higher," a song that she had used as a warm-up for their first recording session.

In the meantime, one of Jackson's records got some attention in Chicago thanks to radio disc jockey Studs Terkel. Terkel first heard Jackson when he wandered into a Chicago record shop on a cold wintry day. The man working behind the counter insisted that Terkel listen to a terrific new record. Then he played Jackson's song "I'm Going to Tell God All About It One of These Days."

Terkel was moved by Jackson's powerful voice. When he discovered that she was from Chicago, he went to hear her sing in a South Side church. Then he introduced her to his radio audience: "There's a woman, my friends, I've seen and heard, who sings like the great blues singer Bessie Smith, only Mahalia Jackson of the South Side doesn't sing the blues. She sings what is known in her church as 'the gospel.'"[1] Then he played her record for the first of many times.

Terkel also invited Jackson to join him on the air during one of his radio broadcasts. Terkel's talents as an interviewer were clear. People enjoyed the lively banter between Jackson and Terkel, and they liked Jackson's music. Terkel would later become noted for his interviews with both celebrities and ordinary people. As host of his own radio show, he went on to interview a variety of well-known guests. He also wrote more than two dozen books, including several oral histories. For these books, he interviewed people about their experiences during particular time periods such as the Great Depression and World War II.

After Jackson's radio interview with Studs Terkel, Berman decided to give Jackson one more try. On September 12, 1947, Jackson and Freeman went back to the studio to record "Move On Up a Little Higher." The song was too long for one side of the record, so they recorded it on two sides as part 1 and part 2. Devoting both sides of a record to one song was something that had not been tried before.

Jackson also had another innovative idea. That was to use both piano and organ as accompaniment. Usually, records featured only one or the other. Jackson believed that the two instruments together would add fullness to the sound.

"Move On Up a Little Higher" was an immediate success. There were so many requests from record stores throughout the country that Apollo had trouble keeping up with demand. Jackson was paid a royalty— a certain percentage of the price of each record sold.

She spent part of the first year's royalties on a Cadillac to use for her tours.

About the time that "Move On Up a Little Higher" was released, Jackson was named official soloist for the National Baptist Convention. Also in 1947, she met pianist Mildred Falls.

Over the years, Jackson had worked with several different accompanists. Not having a regular piano player sometimes left her scrambling to find an accompanist for a concert. The two women first met when Falls was playing for a group of singers who were appearing in the same concert as Jackson. Jackson asked Falls to play for her as well.

"It was a glorious moment," recalled Falls, who had been a fan for years. "I could scarcely believe that I was really playing for the great Mahalia."[2] Soon after that concert, Falls became Jackson's regular accompanist.

They were a strong team, although working with Jackson was not always easy. Jackson often changed the way she sang a song depending on her mood and the response of the audience. Falls learned to adapt to those changes. Over time, it appeared that she could almost anticipate them.

Falls also had to deal with late-night telephone calls. Although Jackson did not read music, she knew how she wanted a song to sound. Inspiration for her music might come to Jackson at any time. Falls sometimes got

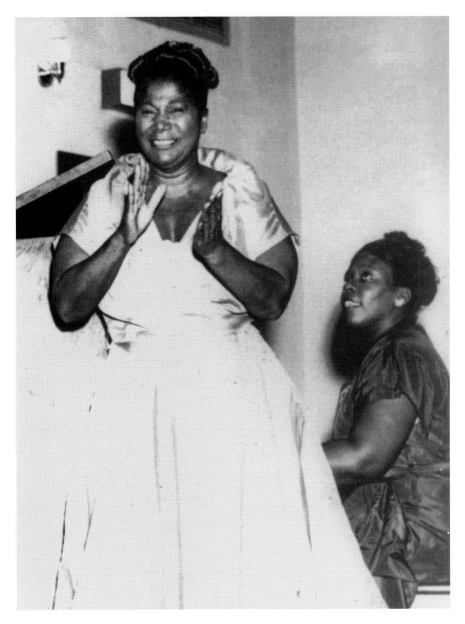

From the time she was a child, pianist Mildred Falls, right, said she was "spellbound" by Jackson's majestic voice and unique style.

calls in the middle of the night when Jackson wanted to talk about an idea for a particular song.

Jackson hired her first agent when Berman introduced her to Harry Lenetska of the William Morris Agency. As her agent, Lenetska would be in charge of organizing concert dates for Jackson. In return, he would get 10 percent of her earnings from those performances. Getting bookings for Jackson was not a problem. In fact, Lenetska had trouble keeping up with all the requests.

With the success of "Move On Up a Little Higher," Berman was eager to release another record. Jackson had already recorded two songs, but she did not agree with Berman about which should be the main side. Berman preferred "What Could I Do," while Jackson liked "Even Me."

Berman produced the record with "What Could I Do" as the hit side and "Even Me" as the flip side. But it was Jackson's favorite, "Even Me," that caught on with listeners around the country.

Even with an agent and successful records, Jackson still had problems with dishonest concert promoters. In 1948, for example, she was asked to sing for a concert at Convention Hall in Philadelphia. When the promoter tried to get out of paying her what she was owed, Jackson took her share of the gate receipts and left. The next morning, the promoter showed up at Jackson's hotel with two policemen. They handcuffed

Jackson and took her to the police station. She called a minister friend, who managed to convince the police that Jackson was entitled to the money she had taken, so she was released.

In 1948, President Harry S. Truman, who was running for reelection, asked Jackson to make some campaign appearances with him. Jackson traveled with Truman, singing at political rallies in Ohio, Missouri, Indiana, and Illinois. Truman was reelected for a second term as president, and in 1949, he invited Jackson to sing at the White House.

That year Jackson sold her beauty salon, but she was still interested in being a businesswoman. She opened another business, Mahalia's House of Flowers. She put friends in charge of running it on a day-to-day basis, but she enjoyed arranging flowers herself when she was in town.

Jackson soon learned that she was developing many European fans. It began with Hugues Pannassie, a French jazz historian. He had a weekly radio program that was broadcast throughout Europe. After discovering Jackson during a trip to New York City, he played her records on his show. His listeners liked her music, and a company that released Apollo's recordings in France and England began distributing Jackson's records in Europe. In 1950, Jackson's recording of "I Can Put My Trust in Jesus" won an award from the French Academy of Music.

That year a concert promoter named Joe Bostic asked Jackson to sing for a gospel concert that he was organizing at Carnegie Hall in New York City. Jackson refused at first, saying that Carnegie Hall was where classically trained musicians performed. "These type of songs [gospel] are not high enough for Carnegie Hall," she insisted.[3] Bostic would not take no for an answer. He continued to ask, and Jackson finally agreed to sing.

The concert was scheduled for October 1, 1950. There were several gospel performers on the program, but Jackson was to have the honor of closing the concert. About eight thousand tickets were sold, many to people from New York City's Harlem. Others had made the trip from cities such as Boston, Pittsburgh, and Raleigh, North Carolina.

Jackson arrived onstage looking elegant in a black velvet choir robe. But she was experiencing a bad case of stage fright. She took a moment to gather her courage. "I stood there gazing out at the thousands of men and women who had come to hear me—a baby nurse and washer woman—on the stage where great artists like [Enrico] Caruso and Lily Pons and Marian Anderson had sung, and I was afraid I wouldn't be able to make a sound," she recalled.[4]

Once she started to sing, all that nervousness was forgotten. Jackson soon had the crowd clapping, stomping their feet, and dancing in the aisles, something that was unheard of at Carnegie Hall. Jackson was so caught up in the music and the audience response that at one point she got down on her knees to sing. It was something she often did when she was feeling the music. Suddenly, Jackson realized where she was. "Now we'd best remember we're in Carnegie Hall," she said to the audience, "and if we cut up too much, they might put us out."[5]

The Chicago Defender reported that Bostic was so excited about the concert that he "immediately announced the affair would be held annually."[6] For the next several years, Jackson performed at each of those yearly concerts.

Most of the people in the audience for the first gospel concert at Carnegie Hall were African Americans. Although Jackson had some successful records, few white people knew about her. That began to change in the early 1950s as new opportunities arose.

One was an invitation from Marshall Stearns, a music professor at Hunter College in New York and a writer about jazz. He was organizing an academic conference on jazz at the Music Inn in Lenox, Massachusetts, and wanted Jackson to participate. Professors from important institutions, including the Juilliard School of Music in New York City, would be there. It was a surprising invitation for Jackson, who did not sing jazz. But the professors were studying the origins of jazz, and they believed that its roots were in

By 1950, Jackson was performing for larger crowds in concert halls.

other types of music such as gospel. Jackson agreed to sing for the group and to talk with the professors about gospel music.

The owners of the Music Inn had done some remodeling. Guests at the conference stayed in what had once been a barn. Jackson was amused to learn that her room had originally been a horse stall. "I finally made it into the white folks' world and look where it landed me!" she joked.[7]

Jackson had been asked to spend one day at the conference, but she ended up staying for the whole week. The professors asked her all kinds of questions, but she just laughed when they tried to analyze her style. They were interested in technical details such as breathing and tone. Jackson was not concerned with those things. "I just told them you're born with singing in you. Everything is right when singing comes from the soul."[8]

Jackson was also asked to perform on Ed Sullivan's *Toast of the Town*, a popular Sunday night television variety show. Television was in its infancy then, and most shows featured only white entertainers. Network executives feared that southern sponsors of the shows would pull their advertising if African Americans appeared on a program. Advertising paid for the shows, and the networks did not want to lose that income. Ed Sullivan was one person who would not be held to that standard. *Toast of the Town* introduced a number of

African Americans to television audiences, including Mahalia Jackson.

On the day Jackson arrived to rehearse for the show, she discovered that she was to be backed up by an orchestra and a choir. Jackson preferred to sing with the accompaniment of only a piano and an organ. She would have to talk to Mr. Sullivan.

People involved with the show knew that Sullivan did not want to be bothered before a show, and no one *ever* disturbed him in his dressing room. Jackson did not listen to their warnings. She marched into his dressing room, surprising Sullivan in his undershorts.

"Don't worry about your shorts," she said. "I'm Mahalia Jackson, and I just came to tell you I don't want all those horns blowin' behind me when I sing. All I want is my piano and my organ and my own way of singing."[9]

Jackson got her way. She performed the song "Dig a Little Deeper" with the accompaniment of only a piano and an organ. Television viewers were delighted. "We got a lot of mail response and they loved her," Sullivan said.[10]

In the meantime, Jackson was making plans for a European tour. Although she had traveled all across the United States, she had never been overseas. Ships made her seasick, and she did not like to fly. "If God meant me to be up there, he wouldn't have put me down here," she explained.[11]

It was the French award for her song "I Can Put My Trust in Jesus" that made her change her mind about going abroad. "If they're going to be nice enough to give me a prize, I ought to be enough of a lady to go and say thank you," she said.[12]

While her agent worked on arrangements for the tour, Jackson continued to perform at concerts in many parts of the country. But she was not feeling well and was losing weight. Her doctor found that she had tumors in her uterus. He advised her to have an operation to remove the uterus, but Jackson said there was no time. She had commitments, including the upcoming European tour. "You'll have a rough trip if you go," her doctor warned.[13] But Jackson would not cancel the tour. People were counting on her.

"Don't you worry 'bout Halie," she said. "I got strength in my mind."[14] She had no way of knowing how much her strength would be tested.

6

A Turning Point

n October 1952, Jackson performed for the third time at Carnegie Hall. Later that month, she left for Europe. Mildred Falls was her accompanist for the tour, and Jackson's agent, Harry Lenetska, traveled with them. The first stop was Paris, where fans gave Jackson such a rousing welcome that the police were needed for crowd control.

Jackson was scheduled for two concerts in two days. It was her custom to read from her Bible backstage to prepare for a performance. But the night of her first concert, she was feeling too weak, so she had her agent read a Bible passage to her. It appeared to give her the strength she needed. Onstage, Jackson performed with the same emotion that audiences had come to expect. She had often moved American audiences to tears during a concert. She got the same response from her fans in France, even though most of them could not understand English. They rewarded her with several curtain calls. The following day, she rested to gain strength for her next performance.

From Paris, she went to London. At her concert in the Royal Albert Hall, she received greetings from Queen Elizabeth and Prime Minister Winston Churchill. Jackson was not the only one on the program for that concert. Others included blues singer Big Bill Broonzy and a jazz band. It did not appear to be a good combination. The hall was only half full, and the audience showed little enthusiasm. Some said that organizers had tried to appeal to too many people by offering three different types of music.

Jackson was not happy with her performance. Not getting the audience involved was a disappointment. But Jackson was weak and in pain. Unknown to the audience, she collapsed offstage. Still, she went on with the tour. Her concerts in the English cities of Southampton, Oxford, and Birmingham went well. Audiences had no idea that Jackson was not in good health.

Jackson gave two concerts in Copenhagen, Denmark. Fans waited outside the auditorium on a cold rainy night just to cheer for Jackson as she left the building. The day after her first concert, children filled her hotel lobby with flowers. On a radio show, Jackson sang her latest European release, "Silent Night." Her appearance on the show brought in twenty thousand mail-order requests for the record.

From Copenhagen, Jackson went back to Paris. She had planned to end her tour with a visit to the Holy Land. That area on the eastern shore of the Mediterranean Sea was said to be where Jesus Christ had lived and died. It was the site of many of the places that Jackson had read about in her Bible.

Jackson got no farther than Paris. She collapsed onstage during a concert and had to cancel the rest of the tour. Doctors said that she was not well enough to travel, but Jackson wanted to be home. Against the doctors' advice, she flew back to Chicago, where she had surgery on November 26.

The surgery dashed any last hopes that Jackson would ever have children. She also faced a slow recovery, after having lost almost ninety pounds in only three months. It took a long while to regain her strength, and Jackson had plenty of time to think about her future. One of the decisions she made was to sell her flower shop.

Jackson's first out-of-town concert after her surgery was in March 1953, when she performed in Muskegon, Michigan. In May, she was back in the recording studio for two new songs, "Down to the River" and "One

Day." By summer, Jackson was back to a full schedule of touring.

In October 1953, Jackson performed at Carnegie Hall again. This time, she stayed in midtown Manhattan at the Wellington Hotel. Until then, African Americans had been banned from hotels in that area of New York City. On past trips, Jackson had stayed in hotels in Harlem and traveled to appointments downtown.

After Mitch Miller of Columbia Records heard Jackson's latest Carnegie Hall concert, he wanted her to sign a contract to record with Columbia. Her current contract with Apollo was coming to an end, and she could sign another, but she was feeling dissatisfied with the company. By that time, "Move On Up a Little Higher" had sold 1.5 million copies. "Even Me" had sold more than a million copies. But Jackson believed that she was not getting her fair share of the earnings from her records.

Jackson decided not to renew her deal with Apollo, but she was in no hurry to sign on with another company. According to some reports, Columbia offered a four-year contract that guaranteed her $50,000 a year, but Jackson wanted time to think about it.

For the next few months, she carried the contract in her oversized purse as she toured the country. She prayed about the offer and pulled the contract out now and then to reread the fine print. She consulted her lawyer in Chicago and asked her friend John Hammond for advice. Hammond was a music critic and record producer. "Mahalia, if you want ads in *Life*, and to be known by the white audience, do it," he said. "But if you want to keep on singing for the black audience, forget signing with Columbia, because they don't know the black market at all."[1] Finally, during Easter week in 1954, Jackson signed the contract.

Afterward, Hammond said that Jackson signed with Columbia for the money. Others said that she was interested in reaching more people through her music. "I believe I have a mission—to sing for people," she had once said.[2] Whatever her reason for going with Columbia, the partnership did help her reach a larger audience. The company moved quickly to promote her.

One of the first things Columbia did was arrange for Jackson to have her own radio show on a CBS radio station in Chicago. At Jackson's request, Studs Terkel was hired as a writer for the show. *The Mahalia Jackson Show* premiered on September 26, 1954. Until then, very few African Americans had hosted their own radio show. Jackson became the first to have one dedicated to gospel music only.

Busy touring, Jackson could not always be in Chicago to do the radio show live on Sunday nights. As a result, the thirty-minute program was taped in front of an audience in a studio theater in the Wrigley Building in downtown Chicago. The theater had

Jackson works with Mitch Miller from Columbia Records in the recording studio.

seating for about four hundred people, and they could not sit quietly once Jackson started to sing. A reporter for *Time* magazine wrote about the first recording session for the show. The audience members cheered and stomped their feet, and Jackson had to quiet them down so that they would not drown out the music. "Don't you start that or we'd tear this studio apart," she scolded. "You got to remember, we're not in church—we're on CBS."[3]

Taping the show in advance also worked well for the show's producers, who were able to cut and shape the program to meet time requirements. That was necessary because Jackson never sang a song the same way twice. For example, her version of "I Believe" was different every time. One day Jackson sang the song in two minutes and forty seconds. Another time she sang it in three minutes and twenty seconds. Such variations were a problem for radio shows. The longer version would cut out two advertisements. The show needed the income from advertisers to stay in business.

In November 1954, Jackson had her first recording session for Columbia Records. By then, record companies were using the new long-playing (LP) records grooved for 33⅓ revolutions per minute (rpm). These LPs could hold about twenty-five minutes of music per side. Jackson recorded fourteen songs for her first album, *Bless This House*. She was backed by the Falls-Jones Ensemble: Mildred Falls on piano, Ralph

Jones on organ, and three other musicians playing guitar, bass, and drums.

Jackson's radio show had a good fan following, but the station had trouble getting sponsors. It ran for only seventeen weeks until February 6, 1955. The last three shows were cut to ten minutes each. After *The Mahalia Jackson Show* was canceled, Jackson began appearing regularly on a local television show called *In Town Tonight*. Studs Terkel was the writer for her appearances.

Jackson continued to tour, and the number of white people in her audiences grew as more of them became familiar with her music. But when Jackson stepped down from the stage, she still faced prejudice. It was confusing. "When I'm on the stage and on television and working with white people, they just hug me and love me, and say I'm so wonderful and I'm so great. And then, when I'm walking down the street like an ordinary citizen, they don't recognize me. And when I go into the department store in the South, they— I can't get a sandwich. I can't get a bottle of pop. I've got to stand. I can't even get a cab. And I'm just the Mahalia Jackson that they got through saying how wonderful I am. I don't understand this. What makes people act like that?" she wondered.[4]

Such prejudice made touring difficult as Jackson and Mildred Falls crisscrossed the country in Jackson's Cadillac. Usually, one of Jackson's relatives drove, but sometimes it was just the two women. There were times

This photo was featured on Jackson's album *Amazing Grace*, for Columbia Records.

when they had to drive all night because blacks were barred from the hotels in the area where they had performed. If they were too tired, they pulled over and slept in the car. They carried fruit with them so they would have something to eat when restaurants refused to serve them.

Falls recalled one night when they stopped at a roadside diner after a concert. She waited in the car while Jackson went to get some food. Jackson soon came back empty-handed, and there were tears in her eyes. She told Falls that a waitress had blocked the door, saying that Jackson could not come in the front. She was ordered to go around to the back door or leave. Jackson refused to use the back door.

The two women were in the car getting ready to pull out of the parking lot when a white truck driver came over to them. "I'm sorry about what happened in there," he said to Jackson. "I hope in my lifetime to see the end of such things."[5] Then he handed them a sack that contained sandwiches and coffee. He left without knowing whom he had helped.

Others were also hoping for an end to prejudice. On December 1, 1955, Rosa Parks, an African-American woman in Montgomery, Alabama, was arrested on a city bus when she refused to give up her seat to a white man. She was not the first to be arrested for that reason, but African-American activists in Montgomery decided to use her arrest to protest segregation by boycotting the city buses. If they stayed off the buses, the bus companies would lose money. Dr. Martin Luther King, Jr., and the Reverend Ralph D. Abernathy helped form the Montgomery Improvement Association (MIA) to aid the boycott. Through this organization, they raised money to organize carpools to get African Americans to work without the buses.

In August 1956, Jackson attended the National Baptist Convention in Denver. It was there that she met the Reverend Abernathy. That fall, he contacted her about coming to Montgomery to sing at a rally to raise money for the bus boycott. He also hoped that Jackson would inspire the people who were getting discouraged with the boycott. It had already lasted months longer than anyone had expected.

7

CIVIL RIGHTS, TELEVISION, AND THE MOVIES

eaders of the Montgomery bus boycott believed in nonviolent protest. India's Mohandas K. Gandhi was their inspiration. He had led a nonviolent movement to help his country gain independence from Great Britain in 1947. Although the Montgomery boycotters believed in peaceful protest, many white people responded to their actions with violence, even bombing Dr. King's home. Abernathy warned Jackson that her life might be in danger in Montgomery, but she still agreed to sing.

Jackson's concert was scheduled for December 6,

1956. By that time, the U.S. Supreme Court had ruled in *Browder* v. *Gayle* that the bus segregation laws were unconstitutional. That ruling had not been put into effect in Montgomery yet, and so the bus boycott continued.

Jackson and Mildred Falls stayed with Reverend Abernathy's family in Montgomery. By noon, people began to crowd into the church where Jackson's concert would be held that evening. The number of people grew so large that loudspeakers were set up in the streets so the overflow could hear her.

That evening, Jackson started her concert with a quiet song, "I've Heard of a City Called Heaven." Her eyes were closed as she sang softly. But before long, she had the audience rocking, and they rose to their feet when she sang "Move On Up a Little Higher." She quieted the crowd by closing the concert with a tribute to the holiday season, "Silent Night."

When Jackson went home, she could feel happy about the turnout and the money raised. But a short time later, the Abernathys' home was bombed. The explosion damaged the living room and the bedroom where Jackson had slept.

The bus boycott finally ended on December 21, 1956. That was when federal injunctions were served on Montgomery, forcing the city to comply with the Supreme Court's ruling.

Northern states did not have segregation laws, but there was racial prejudice. Jackson faced it head-on in 1957 when she tried to buy a house in Chicago. She had saved her money and invested some of it in real estate, including buying the apartment house where she lived. But Jackson liked to practice singing when she was at home, which bothered her neighbors. "Even though they were my tenants," she later wrote, "the people still came flying upstairs to scold me when I sang loud to myself."[1] She believed that in her own house, she would be able to sing whenever she wanted.

In a house, Jackson would also have more room for guests. The apartment was a center of activity with friends coming and going. Often her guests joined her in the kitchen, where she cooked up traditional southern meals. One time, during an interview with a reporter at her apartment, Jackson prepared Creole gumbo, a New Orleans–style stew. "People seem to think it's a little odd for a singer like me to do her own cooking and housework like I do, but this is the real part of me," Jackson told the reporter. "I was doing this long before I ever thought I'd be a singer."[2]

Jackson began her search for a new home by driving through neighborhoods and looking for FOR SALE signs. When she saw one, she would stop to ask about the price. Each time, the white owners would turn her away—claiming that the house had already been sold or that they had changed their mind about selling. Jackson was not prepared for that reaction. It

Even when she was world famous, Jackson loved entertaining guests at home with her southern cooking.

had not occurred to her that she would not be welcome outside the African-American community.

Finally, a real estate agent found a white surgeon willing to sell his home to Jackson. It was a redbrick ranch-style house in a quiet neighborhood. The neighbors were not pleased. Even before she moved in, she received phone calls from people threatening to blow up the house. After she moved in, shots were fired through a front picture window. Jackson was out of town at the time for a concert appearance, but when she got home, she called Mayor Richard Daley. He posted police outside her house for her protection.

The incident received national attention when the well-known journalist Edward R. Murrow asked to interview Jackson at her home. His television show *Person to Person* aired nationally on the CBS network. Jackson used the interview as an opportunity to try to improve her relationship with her neighbors. She invited local children to her house for ice cream and cake during the interview. Many came, but it did not change what had already begun to happen in her neighborhood.

FOR SALE signs started popping up. As each white family moved out, a black family moved in. White people predicted that the neighborhood would turn into a slum, but that did not happen. Lawns remained green and tidy. Houses were well maintained. And children still rode through the neighborhood on their bicycles. Nothing much changed, except the skin color of the residents.

In the meantime, King and Abernathy continued to protest segregation. In 1957, they founded an organization called the Southern Christian Leadership Conference (SCLC). The SCLC was primarily backed by African-American churches, and its goal was to bring about equal rights through nonviolent demonstrations.

The first major event sponsored by the organization was the Prayer Pilgrimage for Freedom, held at the Lincoln Memorial in Washington, D.C., on May 17, 1957. That date was chosen for a special reason. It was the third anniversary of the Supreme Court's *Brown* v. *Board of Education of Topeka* ruling that segregation in public schools was unconstitutional. Outside the Lincoln Memorial, Jackson sang the spiritual "I Been 'Buked and I Been Scorned." Dr. King, the last of fourteen speakers, delivered his first national address.

Also that year, singer Dinah Shore invited Jackson to appear on her television variety show. Over the next few years, Jackson made guest appearances on many television shows. Hosts of some of those programs included the famous singers Bing Crosby and Perry Como and popular comedians Steve Allen, Red Skelton, and Milton Berle. She also made return visits to Ed Sullivan's show and did a guest appearance on Nat "King" Cole's program. Cole was the first African American to have a national television show.

Jackson's voice rang out for civil rights at the Prayer Pilgrimage for
Freedom in 1957.

Jackson had mixed feelings about working on television. One thing she did not like was the time limitation. She was allowed only a certain amount of time for a song. "I'm used to singing in church till the spirit comes. Here they want everything done in two or three minutes," she explained.[3]

Jackson also believed that television producers were trying to change her. "I always got the feeling that some of those producers and studio people were trying to slick me up, turn me into a commercial entertainer," she said.[4]

The good thing about television was that it gave her exposure to a whole new group of people. As Jackson became better known, jazz promoters tried to get her to sing in nightclubs. Some nightclub owners even offered to quit serving drinks while she sang, believing that it was the serving of liquor that kept Jackson from singing in the clubs. But Jackson still turned down their offers. "I have many fine friends who entertain in night clubs and theaters, but it's not the place for my kind of singing," she said.[5]

Jackson did appear at the fourth annual Newport Jazz Festival held in Newport, Rhode Island, in July 1957. She sang during a Sunday afternoon program that was devoted to gospel music. Other performers included the Clara Ward Singers and a group called the Drinkards. Reviewers cited Jackson's performance as a highlight of the festival. "Mahalia Jackson, a woman of immense musical fervor, dominated the afternoon," one critic wrote.[6]

Jackson received another request to sing for a jazz project from her friend Duke Ellington. He wanted her to record a song for his *Black, Brown, and Beige* suite. A suite is a longer work made up of several musical pieces relating to a particular theme. *Black, Brown, and Beige* was Ellington's musical history of African Americans in America.

Ellington first introduced the suite at a concert in Carnegie Hall in 1943. It got a cool reception from both critics and the audience. Over the next few years, Ellington continued to work on the suite, recording some parts of it. In 1956, he decided to expand a spiritual theme that ran throughout the piece. He added lyrics to the fourth section, which he titled "Come Sunday."

Ellington never considered anyone except Jackson to sing the spiritual section. He sent her the music and then followed up with several phone calls to persuade her to do it. Two years passed before they managed to get together to record in Los Angeles with Ellington's orchestra. It was Jackson's first recording with such a large group.

Jackson and Ellington performed the suite at the 1958 Newport Jazz Festival, held during the Fourth of July weekend. Jackson also had her own concert during the festival. It began shortly after midnight on Sunday.

Jackson rehearses for a television special with former football player Rosie Grier.

"Ladies and gentlemen," the master of ceremonies announced, "it is Sunday and it is time for the world's greatest gospel singer, Miss Mahalia Jackson!"[7]

Jackson sang about a dozen songs, including "Didn't It Rain," a lively number about Noah's Ark and the forty days and forty nights of rain. People in the audience clapped and swayed to the music, but there was total silence when she sang "The Lord's Prayer." Some bowed their heads as they listened. Columbia recorded Jackson's concert live. Although some songs were later recorded at a studio with the audience edited in, the album was released as *Live at Newport 1958*.

Jackson also made her film debut in 1958 with a small role in *St. Louis Blues*, starring Nat "King" Cole. In 1959, she played herself singing a gospel song in the movie *Imitation of Life*, starring Lana Turner.

Another highlight for Jackson in 1959 was being invited to sing at the White House for President Dwight D. Eisenhower and the first lady. "Everybody was so nice, and before I was through they were all clapping right with the music," she recalled.[8]

Jackson had often commented that white people in her audiences did not get the clapping right. They clapped *on* the beat instead of *off* the beat. She sometimes joked at her concerts, asking them to stop clapping along with her song. "That's enough darlin's," she would say. "I know you're enjoying yourself, but you just ain't clapping right. If you don't stop, I'm gonna sing something slow."[9]

Jackson had come a long way from the small churches where she had begun her career. But when her spirit needed refueling, she knew where to go. "Those humble churches are my filling stations," she said.[10] By the end of 1959, she was talking about building her own temple.

8

TRAVELING TO THE HOLY LAND

ackson wanted to help future gospel singers and musicians. Part of her plan was to build a temple in Chicago. Although she was a Baptist, she wanted her temple to be for all faiths and all races. She envisioned holding services there that would be broadcast nationally. There would also be music classes and guidance for those interested in a career in gospel music.

Jackson began saving to finance her dream, but there was little time in her schedule to work out the details. She was busy with concerts and recording. In February 1960, she recorded the album *The Power and the Glory* with the Percy Faith Orchestra. Jackson still had doubts about singing with an orchestra, but in the end she liked the album. She also admired Faith's commitment to doing a good job. "One of the best LP's that I've made was with Percy Faith because he is a very strict stern man when you get in the studio. No monkey business," she said.[1]

Others were not as happy with the album. Some of Jackson's fans did not like the way her music had been changing since she signed with Columbia. They felt that her best recordings were her early ones with Apollo, when she sang with only a piano and an organ.

Jackson admitted that she was not entirely happy with her recording company. "One thing I'll say about Columbia is that they put me in a new field," she said. "They got me on TV and they paid me well. The only thing they haven't been too particular about is my songs. I like to sing the songs I feel. They got ideas of what's commercial."[2] At Columbia's urging, she began singing some popular music, such as "Danny Boy," "Summertime," and "Sunrise, Sunset."

Many who heard her in concert thought she sounded much better in person than she did on her records. One reason was that she continued to sing with only a piano and an organ at her concerts. Another reason was that Jackson had such an unforget-table stage presence. "Miss Jackson does not give

"I never had a music lesson and I still can't read music. . . . I just sing it," said Jackson.

concerts; she creates an experience," a reviewer wrote.[3] That experience was a combination of Jackson's strong, rich voice and her belief in the songs she sang.

People told Jackson that they had been healed listening to her music, and for that she was grateful. "You can't reach or uplift people in this way through a mechanical medium such as radio or records or television. Singing directly to a live audience is the only way," she said.[4]

In the spring of 1960, Jackson gave a concert at Constitution Hall in Washington, D.C. In 1939, singer Marian Anderson had been barred from performing in that same hall because she was black. Things were changing, but Jackson knew that there was a long way to go. She continued her work for civil rights.

Jackson had become good friends with Dr. Martin Luther King, Jr. He visited her whenever he was in Chicago, and many civil rights planning sessions were held at her dining table. She also gave concerts to raise bail money for civil rights workers who had been arrested.

In 1960, black college students founded the Student Nonviolent Coordinating Committee (SNCC). They soon came up with a nonviolent way to challenge segregation in public places. Their protests were called sit-ins. The first was in Greensboro, North Carolina. Four African-American students sat at a whites-only lunch counter at a Woolworth's department store. They were refused service, but they did not go away. They sat quietly at the counter until closing time. The next day, they were back, with even more African-American students taking part in the sit-in.

This was just the beginning. Other students began participating in sit-ins as the movement gradually spread to other cities and to other types of businesses, including supermarkets, libraries, and movie theaters. Many of the students were arrested, and many were victims of police brutality. But they did not quit.

In October 1960, the sit-in movement arrived in Atlanta, Georgia, where Dr. King was then living. He was arrested at one of the sit-ins and sentenced to six months in the Georgia State Penitentiary. King's friends and advisers worried about what might happen to him in prison. They turned to the federal government for help.

President Eisenhower and Vice President Richard Nixon both decided not to intervene. At that time, Nixon was campaigning to be elected president. King's advisers contacted the other presidential candidate, U.S. Senator John F. Kennedy. Kennedy asked his brother Robert, who was a lawyer, to look into the situation. Robert Kennedy contacted the judge in Georgia who had sentenced King. The next day, King was free on bond, and a court appeal had been filed. That act won John F. Kennedy much support from

African Americans. He was elected president by a narrow margin in November 1960.

Shortly after Kennedy's election, Jackson was asked to sing "The Star-Spangled Banner" at an inaugural event in Washington, D.C. On January 19, 1961, the day of the event, a blizzard dropped almost eight inches of snow on the city. Traffic slowed to a crawl. The event was delayed to give ticketholders more time to arrive. Although the entertainment started almost two hours late, the evening went on as planned. At a dinner for the cast after the show, Jackson met Kennedy for the first time. She was thrilled when he told her how much he enjoyed her music.

The next day was clear but cold as Jackson sat in wooden bleachers to watch as Kennedy was sworn in as president. She believed that Kennedy would work for an end to segregation, and that gave her hope.

On January 27, 1961, Jackson joined other performers at Carnegie Hall in a concert to raise money for the Southern Christian Leadership Conference (SCLC). Then she and Mildred Falls began a two-month tour of performances throughout the United States. While they traveled, Jackson's agent made arrangements for another European tour. Jackson had been disappointed that illness prevented her from seeing the Holy Land during her first European tour in 1952. She made sure her agent allowed time for a visit to the Holy Land on this trip.

On March 27, Jackson and Falls boarded the S.S. *United States* in New York and set sail for Europe. By now, Jackson had been on the road since late January. She was seasick during the ocean voyage and exhausted from touring. She spent much of the time resting in her cabin. By the time they reached England, she was feeling stronger.

The first stop was London. Jackson appeared on a television show and then prepared for her concert at the Royal Albert Hall. It had been nine years since her last concert there, but the memory was still fresh in her mind. She had been very sick then and had not given a good performance. She prayed this time would be different.

Six thousand people filled the Royal Albert Hall for her concert. Others had to be turned away. They clapped and cheered for Jackson onstage and again after the concert as she exited through the stage door to a waiting car. A reviewer for London's *New Statesman* called her "the most majestic voice of faith" of their generation.[5]

The next day, Jackson sailed across the English Channel and then took a train to Germany. In Frankfurt, she performed at the Kongresshalle. The lighting was poor and the microphones were not working, but the audience was friendly and enthusiastic. Even after twelve encores, the concertgoers cheered for

Jackson rehearses in London during her European tour in 1961.

more. They did not leave until the police showed up to send them on their way.

Jackson's next concert was at the Musikhalle in Hamburg. Then she moved on to East Berlin in East Germany. After World War II, Germany had been split into East Germany and West Germany. East Germany was controlled by Communists. Under this type of government, people are not allowed to own property, so the government seized land, banks, and businesses. The Communist government ruled by force. When Jackson arrived, armed soldiers were policing the streets to keep citizens from protesting against the government or escaping to West Berlin. They checked Jackson's papers as she entered the city.

It was Jackson's first trip into a Communist country, and the soldiers made her uneasy. She had heard stories about people disappearing after protesting against communism. The presence of the soldiers made those stories seem real, but they did not have an effect on Jackson's concert. Seats in the Sportspalast were filled, and some audience members stood on balcony steps or sat on the floor. While armed soldiers and tanks patrolled the streets outside the hall, the crowd inside was quiet as Jackson sang "Let There Be Peace on Earth." When she finished, they stood and shouted their approval. The manager told her that he had not heard such cheering since the Nazi dictator Adolf Hitler spoke there in 1938. His words made

Jackson shiver. "I shuddered to think that Hitler had stood there and cried for war," she later wrote.[6]

Jackson was only partway through her tour, but already the concerts and the travel between locations were wearing her down. Although she did not like to fly, she felt it was necessary now so she could save her energy for her concerts. Flying would take less time than traveling by train, giving her more time to rest in her hotel rooms. The day after the Sportspalast concert, she boarded a plane for Copenhagen, Denmark.

People in Europe were aware of the civil rights movement in the United States. A reporter in Copenhagen asked Jackson about it. Did she feel she was treated unfairly in America because of her race? Jackson knew that the reporter hoped to get a juicy quote, but she would not say anything against her country. She told the reporter that she had experienced many hard times in her life, but they were not related to the color of her skin.

Columbia recorded Jackson's concert in Stockholm, Sweden, for release later as a live album. From there, Jackson traveled to the Netherlands for a concert in Amsterdam. She went on to Paris and back to Germany for concerts in Munich and Essen. Her final European concert was in Zurich, Switzerland.

In Rome, Jackson had an audience with the pope. Then she went by train to Naples, where she boarded a ship bound for the Holy Land. She had only one concert scheduled there, in Tel Aviv, Israel. Until then, she could go sightseeing.

The ship docked in Beirut, Lebanon. From there, Jackson went to Damascus, Syria, where she began her journey to Jerusalem by car. The driver assigned to her was a large Arab man. Jackson called him "Fez" because he wore a red fez—a felt hat shaped like a cone with a flat top instead of a point. Fez drove fast, and the road was bumpy and narrow. Jackson held on with one hand and used the other one to poke Fez when she wanted him to slow down. "We went racing down through the desert with me poking and hollering and him telling me he had never been treated that way before by any woman and he would like to come to the United States and marry me," Jackson recalled.[7] Jackson told him she would not marry such a bad driver.

They stopped at the River Jordan, then journeyed past Jericho. There Jackson was reminded of the biblical story in which Joshua brings the walls of Jericho down with a mighty shout from his men.

The next day, Jackson visited several places she had read about in the Bible, including Bethlehem, the Garden of Gethsemane, and Old Jerusalem. She knelt and prayed in the church near Calvary, the hill outside ancient Jerusalem where Jesus was crucified and died. "My dreams have come true," she said quietly.[8] She had finally seen some of the sacred places that she had read about in her Bible and sang about in her music.

Then it was on to the concert in Tel Aviv. More than two thousand people crowded into the auditorium. Some were Christians and some were Jews. Most of them could not understand English, but none of the differences appeared to matter. Everyone was captivated by Jackson's performance. "When she got to 'Joshua Fit [Fought] the Battle of Jericho,' the walls of the auditorium almost came down," wrote a reporter for *Time* magazine.[9]

After the program, Jackson went home to Chicago. At that time, the civil rights movement was entering a new phase.

9

LOVE AND LOSS

n 1956, the U.S. Supreme Court ruled that buses and other forms of interstate transportation could not be segregated. But in practice, there was still a "whites only" policy in some areas. In May 1961, a group of activists who called themselves Freedom Riders decided to challenge segregation on interstate buses. The Freedom Riders, made up of both blacks and whites, bought tickets for buses traveling through states in the South. At bus terminals, blacks sat down for service at whites-only lunch counters, and they used restrooms designated for white people.

In some cities there were no problems, but in others the Freedom Riders encountered violence. In Anniston, Alabama, whites chased after a bus and flung a bomb through a window, setting the bus on fire. As the Freedom Riders hurried off the bus to escape the flames, some of them were grabbed and beaten by the mob. Angry whites also attacked Freedom Riders in Montgomery, Alabama, setting one African-American man on fire. Police used tear gas to bring that riot to an end.

Jackson was not directly involved in these protests, but she did what she could in the fight for equal rights. She sang to raise money for the civil rights movement, participating in a large fund-raiser for the Southern Christian Leadership Conference (SCLC) in Los Angeles during the summer of 1961. She also continued to tour. "I have hopes that my singing will break down some of the hate and fear that divide the white and black people in this country," she said.[1]

Jackson was reaching new milestones with her music. In 1962, the National Academy of Recording Arts and Sciences added a new category to their Grammy Awards—gospel. Jackson was the first to receive that award. On October 13, 1962, she became the first gospel artist to perform at New York's Philharmonic Hall. In 1963, Jackson won another Grammy Award for her album *Great Songs of Love and Faith.*

Jackson displays her many awards on her piano. The photo shows Jackson and Nat "King" Cole in a scene from the movie *St. Louis Blues*.

In the spring of 1963, Jackson organized an SCLC benefit in Chicago. She persuaded musicians, entertainers, stagehands, and ushers to volunteer their services. Every penny was to be donated to SCLC. Mayor Richard Daley agreed to let her use the Arie Crown Theatre in the McCormick Place Convention Center free of charge. Although African Americans would later criticize Daley for not being a strong supporter of civil rights, he was a good friend to

Jackson. Martin Luther King, Jr., spoke to the crowd of more than five thousand cheering people, and Jackson sang.

Soon plans were under way for the March on Washington for Jobs and Freedom to be held in Washington, D.C., in August 1963. President John F. Kennedy had sent his proposed civil rights bill to Congress in June. Organizers of the march wanted people to come to Washington to show their support for even stronger civil rights legislation. King asked Jackson to participate in what would be a most memorable day, with her singing followed by his "I Have a Dream" speech.

Some people had predicted that the day would be marred by racial riots. All the officers on the Washington, D.C., police force were on duty that day. There were additional policemen brought in from other communities to help. But as the marchers gathered at the Washington Monument, it looked more like a scene from a county fair. People were picnicking, talking, and singing. About two hundred thousand people marched to the Lincoln Memorial, but there was no violence. "It was as if the human race had taken a day off from being mean to each other," Jackson noted.[2]

A day that ended in triumph was soon followed by tragedy. Less than three weeks later, whites bombed an African-American church in Birmingham, Alabama.

Four young African-American girls were killed. Two months later, on November 22, 1963, President John F. Kennedy was shot and killed as he rode in a motorcade through Dallas, Texas.

Jackson was in Los Angeles rehearsing for a television special for CBS when she heard the news of Kennedy's assassination. The rehearsal was canceled, and she went back to her hotel room. She cried as she watched the news coverage.

In the meantime, CBS was hurriedly putting together a special program about Kennedy, and Jackson was asked to participate. Only hours after Kennedy's death, she sang "Nearer My God to Thee" on national television, while tears rolled down her cheeks.

Jackson had never wavered in her admiration for Kennedy and in her belief that he was an ally for civil rights. With his death, Vice President Lyndon B. Johnson was sworn in as president. He vowed to continue to work for the civil rights legislation that Kennedy had proposed to Congress earlier that year.

Jackson later said that one of the people who helped her through the sadness she felt after Kennedy's death was Sigmund Galloway. Jackson had met Galloway about a year earlier when she was in California recording an album. Galloway was immediately taken with Jackson when he heard her sing. "I thought to myself, a woman who can sing like that must be very warm inside," he said.[3]

Galloway was originally from Indiana and had sold real estate in the Chicago area until 1951. Then he moved to California with hopes of jump-starting a music career. He played flute, clarinet, and saxophone, and had studied music in Chicago before going into real estate. Jackson had known Galloway's family in Indiana when he was married. When Jackson saw him in California, he was a widower with a young daughter.

Galloway and Jackson began spending time together whenever she was in Los Angeles, which was often. Columbia Records had moved its recording studios from New York to California, and many of the television shows Jackson appeared on were filmed there. She had bought a sixteen-unit apartment building in the area as an investment and also as a place to stay when she was in Los Angeles. Her younger half-brother managed the building for her. Galloway also visited Jackson in Chicago.

Jackson had a full life with her career and friends, and since her divorce from Hockenhull, she had never remarried. She often joked about that with her audiences. "Surely out of all these handsome men," she would say, "I can find me a good husband."[4]

Although she joked about it, she was lonely. "I have nobody to come home to," she said. "At my age a person misses these things more and more."[5]

In 1964, Jackson left for a month-long European tour. On the way home, she thought about her future and about Galloway. He was talking about marriage, and Jackson decided she was ready for that step. They were married on July 2, 1964, in a small private ceremony. The only people present were Jackson's secretary, who served as matron of honor, and her manager, the best man. Galloway was forty-seven years old, and Jackson was fifty-one.

On that same day, President Lyndon B. Johnson signed the Civil Rights Act of 1964. The act made segregation illegal in restaurants, hotels, and other public places. It also protected people from discrimination by employers, and it stated that voting requirements for blacks must be the same as those for whites. In some areas, discriminatory voting requirements for African Americans had prevented them from voting.

Later that year, *Ebony* magazine published a story about Galloway and Jackson and their July wedding. It painted a cozy picture of the couple at home. Photos showed them in the kitchen doing dishes together, and Jackson working in her garden. There were also photos of Jackson with Galloway's five-year-old daughter, Sigma. It appeared that Jackson finally had the family she had always wanted.

Still, not everyone was happy to see Jackson married. Soon after the announcement of their wedding, Jackson began receiving letters from people who feared that her marriage would interfere with her work. Jackson's friends, who had been frequent visitors in her home, felt that Galloway did not want them around. So they began to stay away.

Although Jackson tried to reassure her friends and fans, she also had concerns about her marriage. Jackson soon realized that some of the things that had first attracted her to Galloway became problems after they were married. "This very thing that I loved in him, his gayety and his zest for living, became an obsession with him after we were married," Jackson recalled. "He wanted to go some place every night, but I wasn't used to that. My body had to have rest."[6]

Two months after their wedding, Jackson was hospitalized after having a heart attack. She would be admitted to the hospital several times over the next two years. She was diagnosed with diabetes and heart problems. In addition to her physical ailments, Jackson was also sick at heart. She knew that her marriage was not a good one, but she kept her feelings to herself. "He [Galloway] was unhappy and I was sick," Jackson later said. "I had made a mistake, but I did not want people to know that I had made such a fool of myself."[7]

Another problem in their marriage was Jackson's career. She understood that some men found it hard to be married to a successful woman. She allowed Galloway to take an active role in her career, including doing arrangements for some of her songs. She also tried to help Galloway with his music career. She introduced him to her contacts in the business and even convinced Columbia to record him. When his career did not take off as he hoped, he became angry and critical of Jackson.

Jackson was especially hurt that he criticized her grammar when she did interviews with the press. She had once been embarrassed about her lack of formal education, but she no longer felt that people judged her because of it. "I am not an educated woman," she said. "I'm just myself and the world has accepted me as I am."[8]

Jackson continued working and acted as if everything was fine with her marriage. On October 7, 1965, she sang for President Lyndon B. Johnson at a concert in Washington, D.C. At the White House, Jackson, Galloway, and Mildred Falls posed for photos with the president and first lady. But it would be one of Jackson's last performances with Falls as her accompanist.

It is not clear exactly what happened between Jackson and Falls. One explanation came from Brother John Sellers, whom Jackson had taken in as a boy. She had helped him launch his career in music, and she and Sellers had remained friends over the years. Sellers was critical of the way Jackson held on to her money, saying she was too selfish. "Mahalia was the type of woman who wouldn't pay anybody if she could

Jackson performed for President Lyndon B. Johnson in Washington, D.C. Pictured, from left to right, are Mildred Falls, Jackson's husband Sigmund Galloway, First Lady Lady Bird Johnson, Mahalia Jackson, President Lyndon B. Johnson, and Edward Robinson, who accompanied Jackson on the organ.

keep from doing it," Sellers noted. "That's how she got rich and kept her money."[9] Sellers said Jackson fired Falls after the accompanist asked for a raise.

Others believed that Galloway had come between Jackson and Falls. They said that he wanted to control Jackson's career and wanted Falls out of the way. Still others said that Falls was forced to retire for health reasons. She had arthritis, and touring had become too hard for her.

Jackson continued touring and supporting civil rights. In 1966, Chicago, like many other cities across the United States, was plagued with race riots. In spite of the Civil Rights Act of 1964, racism still existed. African Americans who tried to move from ghettos into white neighborhoods faced the same kind of prejudice that Jackson had met when she bought her home in 1957. That was a problem that Martin Luther King, Jr., addressed in Chicago during the summer of 1966.

Jackson helped organize a large freedom rally in Chicago held on July 10. With temperatures soaring into the nineties, about sixty thousand people gathered at Soldier Field. Jackson sang and King spoke. After the rally, five thousand people, including Jackson, marched to City Hall. King taped a copy of their demands for open housing on a door of the building.

There were other protests throughout the summer as blacks marched into white neighborhoods. One observer recalled a march on August 5, which Jackson helped lead. Whites threw rocks, bricks, and bottles at the marchers, hitting King in the face with a brick. But King marched on, and so did Jackson. She knew from her own experience how hurtful it was to be barred from a neighborhood because of race.

That year, Jackson and Galloway separated; it was the first step in a messy divorce. Jackson owned the house, but she had moved out to avoid some of the unpleasantness of their marriage. With a divorce pending, she felt that Galloway should be the one to leave. Galloway refused, and Jackson spent three months living in hotels. She eventually got her home back, and the friends who had stayed away during her marriage began to return. The divorce was finalized in April 1967.

That month, she sang at an Easter concert in New York's Philharmonic Hall. People said that she was not herself at that concert. She looked frail and sang in a surprisingly quiet voice. With the stress of her divorce, Jackson had lost weight and was down to about one hundred sixty pounds. It was a healthy weight for her heart, but she was more comfortable at about two hundred pounds, which she considered her singing weight.

By summer, Jackson had gained back some of the lost weight and some of her old energy. At a concert in Oakland, California, she told the audience that they were her family. "I've been serving you for thirty years," she said. "I'm married to you, not to that man."[10] Then she sang a rousing version of "How I Got Over."

That year, Jackson left for another European tour that was to include concerts in West Germany, Britain, Switzerland, and Italy. Unfortunately, she got no farther than West Germany. She collapsed backstage in Berlin and was hospitalized for what was said to be exhaustion. She canceled the rest of the tour and returned to Chicago to rest.

On April 4, 1968, Jackson's world was again shattered when Martin Luther King, Jr., was assassinated in Memphis, Tennessee. Jackson sang "Precious Lord, Take My Hand" at his funeral service in Atlanta, Georgia. "I think she sang more beautifully than I had ever heard her sing before," Dr. King's widow, Coretta Scott King, noted.[11]

Two months later, on June 5, Senator Robert F. Kennedy was shot while he was in Los Angeles campaigning for the Democratic nomination for the presidency. He died the next day. Once again, Jackson put aside her own sadness long enough to appear on CBS television to sing in his honor.

After King's death, Jackson was not as active in the civil rights movement. She focused on charitable work, such as raising money for churches. She continued to make plans to build her temple in Chicago, but there were too many roadblocks in finding a location and getting funding. In the end, she was not able to achieve that dream, but she did provide scholarships for college students through the Mahalia Jackson Foundation. She also continued to tour in the United States and overseas.

10

A STAR
THAT CONTINUES
TO SHINE

n the spring of 1971, Jackson traveled to
Japan as an unofficial goodwill ambassador
for the U.S. government. In Toyko, she sang
at the Imperial Palace for Emperor Hirohito in honor
of his seventieth birthday. From there, she went to
India, where she gave a three-hour concert. Prime
Minister Indira Gandhi was late for a meeting because
she did not want to leave the concert early.

At the U.S. government's request, Jackson returned
to Europe in September 1971 to entertain American
troops in Germany. There were problems between
black and white American soldiers stationed there.

Mahalia Jackson

"I have hopes that my singing will break down some of the hate and fear that divide the white and black people in this country," said Mahalia Jackson, whose heartfelt performances often moved audiences to tears.

Government officials hoped that Jackson would be able to calm some of the tension with her music. Unfortunately, she fell ill almost immediately and was hospitalized. She had to be flown back to Chicago on an army medical evacuation plane.

During the next few months, Jackson was in and out of the hospital several times. On January 27, 1972, she died of heart failure in Evergreen Park, Illinois, a few days after abdominal surgery. She was fifty-nine.

At the Greater Salem Baptist Church in Chicago, more than forty thousand people filed past Jackson's coffin to pay their respects. Because such a large crowd was expected for the funeral service, it was held at the Arie Crown Theater. It had seating for about five thousand.

At the service, Thomas A. Dorsey read a poem that he had written, and Coretta Scott King spoke about how much her husband had enjoyed Jackson's music. He had said that "a voice like this comes, not once a century, but once a millennium."[1] Jackson's friend Robert Anderson sang "Move On Up a Little Higher." He was accompanied by Mildred Falls, whose arthritis was so bad by that time that she had to be helped to the piano. The Reverend C. L. Franklin preached at the service, and his daughter, Aretha Franklin, sang "Precious Lord, Take My Hand."

Jackson's body was flown to New Orleans, where it again lay in state as an estimated sixty thousand mourners filed past. After another large funeral service, Jackson was buried at Providence Memorial Park in a suburb of New Orleans.

Shortly after her death, Jackson was honored with a Lifetime Achievement Grammy Award. On May 6, 1997, she was inducted into the Rock and Roll Hall of Fame in Cleveland, and on July 15, 1998, she was honored with a stamp issued by the U.S. Postal Service. It was a part of a collection of stamps honoring women in gospel music.

As a child in New Orleans, Jackson was surrounded by music—blues, jazz, the hymns of her Baptist church, and the rhythms of the Pentecostal church. All of those influences became part of her unique style of gospel music. She sang gospel when people said it would not sell, and she made it popular.

Jackson sang for four American presidents and for royalty throughout the world, but she was happiest when she was singing for people in small churches. She sang to people of all nationalities and of all faiths. During the civil rights movement, both blacks and whites embraced her music, forgetting their differences at least for a while. "When she finished singing, there was no hatred," one observer noted.[2]

Today people still enjoy her songs, which have been reissued on compact discs. More than thirty years after her death, Jackson's music continues to touch the hearts and lift the spirits of listeners throughout the world.

CHRONOLOGY

1912—Born October 26 in New Orleans, Louisiana.

1927—Moves to Chicago.

1929—Begins singing professionally with a group known as the Johnson Gospel Singers.

1936—Marries Isaac "Ike" Hockenhull.

1937—Records four songs for Decca Records.

1939—Opens Mahalia's Beauty Salon.

1943—Divorces Hockenhull.

1946—Signs a recording contract with Apollo Records.

1947—Her recording "Move On Up a Little Higher" becomes an immediate success; is named official soloist for the National Baptist Convention; meets Mildred Falls, who soon became her longtime accompanist.

1949—President Harry S. Truman invites her to sing at the White House; opens Mahalia's House of Flowers.

1950—Receives an award from the French Academy of Music; sings at Carnegie Hall.

1952—Tours Europe for the first time.

1954—Signs with Columbia Records; *The Mahalia Jackson Show* premiers on CBS radio in Chicago.

1956—Meets the Reverend Martin Luther King, Jr., and becomes involved with the civil rights movement.

1957—Experiences racial prejudice when she buys a home in a white community in Chicago; sings at the Prayer Pilgrimage for Freedom at the Lincoln Memorial in Washington, D.C.; performs at the Newport Jazz Festival in Newport, Rhode Island.

1958—Records *Black, Brown, and Beige* with Duke Ellington; performs with Ellington at the Newport Jazz Festival; makes film debut in *St. Louis Blues.*

1959—Appears in the film *Imitation of Life*; performs at the White House for President Dwight D. Eisenhower.

1960—Records *The Power and the Glory* with the Percy Faith Orchestra; sings at Constitution Hall in Washington, D.C.

1961—Performs at an inauguration event for president-elect John F. Kennedy; completes a second European tour.

1962—Is the first to win a Grammy Award for the new gospel category; is the first gospel singer to perform at New York's Philharmonic Hall.

1963—Performs at the March on Washington for Jobs and Freedom.

1964—Marries Sigmund Galloway.

1965—Performs for President Lyndon B. Johnson.

1967—Divorces Sigmund Galloway; is hospitalized in West Berlin when she collapses backstage.

1968—Sings at a funeral service for Martin Luther King, Jr.

1971—Travels to India and Japan.

1972—Dies in a Chicago hospital on January 27; is awarded a Lifetime Achievement Grammy Award.

1997—Inducted into the Rock and Roll Hall of Fame.

1998—Is honored with a stamp issued by the U.S. Postal Service.

SELECTED DISCOGRAPHY

Black Brown & Beige. Columbia Legacy, 1999. Recorded with Duke Ellington in 1958. Extra tracks have been added to this edition.

Mahalia Jackson: Gospels, Spirituals, & Hymns. Columbia Legacy, 1998. This two-disc set includes many of Jackson's best-known gospel songs including "Didn't It Rain," "Move On Up a Little Higher," and "His Eye Is on the Sparrow." Also included are two previously unreleased songs.

Mahalia Jackson: Live at Newport, 1958. Columbia Legacy, 1994. Jackson's concert at the 1958 Newport Jazz Festival in Newport, Rhode Island. Some songs were later redone in a studio. Includes "Didn't It Rain," "He's Got the Whole World in His Hands," "I'm Going to Live the Life I Sing About in My Song," and "The Lord's Prayer."

Mahalia Jackson: Recorded in Europe During Her Latest Concert Tour. Columbia Legacy, 2001. Recorded live during Jackson's tour in 1961. This recording has been remastered with extra tracks added. Songs include "You'll Never Walk Alone," "How I Got Over," and "When the Saints Go Marching In."

The Power and the Glory. Columbia Legacy, 1998. An album of Jackson's favorite hymns originally recorded with Percy Faith and his orchestra in 1960.

CHAPTER NOTES

Chapter 1. "I Been 'Buked and I Been Scorned"

1. "Big Day—End and a Beginning," *Newsweek*, September 9, 1963, p. 20.

2. Alden Whitman, "Mahalia Jackson, Gospel Singer and a Civil Rights Symbol, Dies," *The New York Times*, January 28, 1972, p. 1.

3. Russell Baker, "Capital Is Occupied by a Gentle Army," *The New York Times*, August 29, 1963, p. 17.

4. Jules Schwerin, *Got To Tell It: Mahalia Jackson, Queen of Gospel* (New York: Oxford University Press, 1992), p. 144.

5. Baker, p. 17.

Chapter 2. A Small Girl with a Big Voice

1. Mahalia Jackson as told to Evan McLeod Wylie, "I Can't Stop Singing," *The Saturday Evening Post*, December 5, 1959, p. 20.

2. Ibid.

3. Jules Schwerin, *Got To Tell It: Mahalia Jackson, Queen of Gospel* (New York: Oxford University Press, 1992), p. 21.

4. Mahalia Jackson, "Make a Joyful Noise!" *Music Journal*, January 1965, p. 72.

5. Studs Terkel, *Talking to Myself: A Memoir of My Times* (New York: Pantheon Books, 1977), p. 261.

6. Schwerin, p. 30.

7. Mahalia Jackson with Evan McLeod Wylie, *Movin' On Up* (New York: Hawthorn Books, Inc., 1966), p. 33.

8. Terkel, p. 262.

9. *I Sing Because I'm Happy: An Interview with Songs with Mahalia Jackson, Vol. 1*, LP, recorded, annotated, and

compiled by Jules Schwerin (New York: Folkways Records & Service Corp., 1979).

10. *I Sing Because I'm Happy: An Interview with Songs with Mahalia Jackson, Vol. 2*, LP, recorded, annotated, and compiled by Jules Schwerin (New York: Folkways Records & Service Corp., 1979).

11. *Mahalia Jackson Discusses Movin' On Up with Columnist Robert Cromie* (Educational Research Group, Inc., 1969), audiocassette.

12. Mildred Falls, "Unforgettable Mahalia Jackson," *Reader's Digest*, March 1974, p. 103.

Chapter 3. A New Start

1. Mahalia Jackson with Evan McLeod Wylie, *Movin' On Up* (New York: Hawthorn Books, Inc., 1966), p. 38.

2. Ibid., p. 42.

3. Mahalia Jackson as told to Evan McLeod Wylie, "I Can't Stop Singing," *The Saturday Evening Post*, December 5, 1959, p. 21.

4. Ibid.

5. *Movin' On Up*, p. 47.

6. *Mahalia Jackson Discusses Movin' On Up with Columnist Robert Cromie* (Educational Research Group, Inc., 1969), audiocassette.

7. Laurraine Goreau, *Just Mahalia, Baby* (Waco, Texas: Word Books, Publisher, 1975), p. 55.

8. Ibid.

9. *Movin' On Up*, p. 51.

10. Michael W. Harris, *The Rise of Gospel Blues: The Music of Thomas Andrew Dorsey in the Urban Church* (New York: Oxford University Press, 1992), p. 258.

11. Ibid.

12. Henry Pleasants, *The Great American Popular Singers* (New York: Simon & Schuster, 1974), p. 208.

13. *Movin' On Up*, p. 59.

14. *Mahalia: Give God the Glory!* (Onyx Films, Inc., 1988), videocassette.

Chapter 4. A "Fish-and-Bread" Singer

1. Laurraine Goreau, *Just Mahalia, Baby* (Waco, Texas: Word Books, Publisher, 1975), p. 57.

2. Mahalia Jackson, "I Sing for the Lord," *Music Journal*, January 1963, p. 19.

3. Mahalia Jackson with Evan McLeod Wylie, *Movin' On Up* (New York: Hawthorn Books, Inc., 1966), p. 61.

4. Goreau, p. 66.

5. *I Sing Because I'm Happy: An Interview with Songs with Mahalia Jackson, Vol. 2*, LP, recorded, annotated, and compiled by Jules Schwerin (New York: Folkways Records & Service Corp., 1979).

6. Goreau, p. 75.

7. Mahalia Jackson as told to Evan McLeod Wylie, "I Can't Stop Singing," *The Saturday Evening Post*, December 5, 1959, p. 98.

8. Mahalia Jackson, "Marital Bliss vs. Single Blessedness," *Ebony*, April 1968, p. 96.

9. Goreau, p. 79.

10. "When Mahalia Sings," *Ebony*, January 1954, p. 38.

Chapter 5. "Move On Up a Little Higher"

1. Jules Schwerin, *Got To Tell It: Mahalia Jackson, Queen of Gospel* (New York: Oxford University Press, 1992), p. 64.

2. Mildred Falls, "Unforgettable Mahalia Jackson," *Reader's Digest*, March 1974, p. 103.

3. Laurraine Goreau, *Just Mahalia, Baby* (Waco, Texas: Word Books, Publisher, 1975), p. 131.

4. Mahalia Jackson with Evan McLeod Wylie, *Movin' On Up* (New York: Hawthorn Books, Inc., 1966), pp. 90–91.

5. Ibid., p. 91.

6. "8,000 Witness First Negro Gospel Concert," *The Chicago Defender*, October 14, 1950, p. 21.

7. *Movin' On Up*, p. 88.

8. "Born to Sing," *Newsweek*, February 22, 1954, p. 98.

9. Falls, p. 104.

10. Goreau, p. 153.

11. Irving Townsend, CD program notes, *The Power and the Glory* (Columbia Legacy, 1998).

12. Don Gold, "In God She Trusts," *Ladies' Home Journal*, November 1963, p. 67.

13. Goreau, p. 162.

14. Ibid.

Chapter 6. A Turning Point

1. Henry Pleasants, *The Great American Popular Singers* (New York: Simon & Schuster, 1974), p. 210.

2. Don Gold, "In God She Trusts," *Ladies' Home Journal*, November 1963, p. 67.

3. "Gospel with a Bounce," *Time*, October 4, 1954, p. 46.

4. Studs Terkel, *Four Decades with Studs Terkel: A Compilation of Extraordinary Interviews from 40 Years of Broadcasting* (St. Paul, Minn.: HighBridge Company, 1993), audiocassette, Tape One, Side B.

5. Mildred Falls, "Unforgettable Mahalia Jackson," *Reader's Digest*, March 1974, p. 104.

Chapter 7. Civil Rights, Television, and the Movies

1. Mahalia Jackson with Evan McLeod Wylie, *Movin' On Up* (New York: Hawthorn Books, Inc., 1966), p. 119.

2. Carlton Brown, "A Joyful Noise," *Harper's Magazine*, August 1956, p. 82.

3. Anthony Heilbut, *The Gospel Sound: Good News and Bad Times* (New York: Limelight Edition, 1997), p. 68.

4. Jules Schwerin, *Got To Tell It: Mahalia Jackson, Queen of Gospel* (New York: Oxford University Press, 1992), p. 106.

5. Brown, p. 84.

6. Nat Hentoff, "The Newport Jazz Festival Blues," *Saturday Review*, July 20, 1957, p. 29.

7. *Jazz on a Summer's Day* (New York: Raven Films, 1987), videocassette.

8. Irving Townsend, CD program notes, *The Power and the Glory* (Columbia Legacy, 1998).

9. Hettie Jones, *Big Star Fallin' Mama: Five Women in Black Music*, rev. ed. (New York: Penguin Books USA, Inc., 1995), pp. 58–59.

10. Alex Haley, "She Makes a Joyful Music," *Reader's Digest*, November 1961, p. 202.

Chapter 8. Traveling to the Holy Land

1. *Mahalia Jackson Discusses Movin' On Up with Columnist Robert Cromie* (Educational Research Group, Inc., 1969), audiocassette.

2. Nat Hentoff, "You Can Still Hear Her Voice When the Music Has Stopped," *The Reporter*, June 27, 1957, p. 36.

3. Whitney Balliett, "Heaven and Earth," *The New Yorker*, April 8, 1967, p. 165.

4. Mahalia Jackson, "Make a Joyful Noise!" *Music Journal*, January 1965, p. 72.

5. Francis Newton, "Mahalia," *New Statesman*, April 14, 1961, p. 598.

6. Mahalia Jackson with Evan McLeod Wylie, *Movin' On Up* (New York: Hawthorn Books, Inc., 1966), p. 155.

7. Ibid., p. 165.

8. E. M. Wylie, "I Walked in Jerusalem," *Good Housekeeping*, December 1961, p. 136.

9. "Joyful Noise in Israel," *Time*, May 26, 1961, p. 81.

Chapter 9. Love and Loss

1. Alden Whitman, "Mahalia Jackson, Gospel Singer and a Civil Rights Symbol, Dies," *The New York Times*, January 28, 1972, p. 56.

2. Mahalia Jackson with Evan McLeod Wylie, *Movin' On Up* (New York: Hawthorn Books, Inc., 1966), p. 192.

3. Era Bell Thompson, "Love Comes to Mahalia," *Ebony*, November 1964, p. 54.

4. Anthony Heilbut, *The Gospel Sound: Good News and Bad Times* (New York: Limelight Edition, 1997), p. 64.

5. "Gospel in Washington," *Newsweek*, April 4, 1960, p. 68.

6. Mahalia Jackson, "Marital Bliss vs. Single Blessedness," *Ebony*, April 1968, p. 90.

7. Ibid., p. 94.

8. Ibid., p. 96.

9. Jules Schwerin, *Got To Tell It: Mahalia Jackson, Queen of Gospel* (New York: Oxford University Press, 1992), p. 120.

10. Heilbut, p. 71.

11. Coretta Scott King, *My Life with Martin Luther King, Jr.* (New York: Holt, Rinehart, and Winston, 1969), p. 332.

Chapter 10. A Star That Continues to Shine

1. George Vecsey, "Thousands Mourn Mahalia Jackson," *The New York Times*, February 2, 1972, p. 42.

2. Charles-Gene McDaniel, "Funeralizing Mahalia," *The Christian Century*, March 1, 1972, p. 254.

FURTHER READING

Donloe, Darlene. *Mahalia Jackson: Gospel Singer*. Los Angeles: Melrose Square Publishing Company, 1992.

Gourse, Leslie. *Mahalia Jackson: Queen of Gospel Song*. New York: Franklin Watts, 1996.

Jackson, Mahalia, with Evan McLeod Wylie. *Movin' On Up*. New York: Hawthorn Books, 1966.

Orgill, Roxane. *Mahalia: A Life in Gospel Music*. Cambridge, Mass.: Candlewick Press, 2002.

Wolfe, Charles K. *Mahalia Jackson: Gospel Singer*. New York: Chelsea House Publishers, 1990.

INTERNET ADDRESSES

< http://www.galegroup.com/free_resources/bhm/bio/jackson_m.htm >
This informative, easy-to-read biography also includes a list of resources for additional information.

< http://www.rockhall.com/hof/inductee.asp?id=126 >
This site spotlights Jackson's induction into the Rock and Roll Hall of Fame. It includes a short biography and a timeline of important events in her life.

< http://www.nytimes.com/learning/general/onthisday/bday/1026.html >
This site features a story written by Alden Whitman for *The New York Times* at the time of Jackson's death. It includes biographical information as well as background on her civil rights work. The site also includes a short editorial examining Jackson's contribution to gospel music.

INDEX

Pages with photographs are in **boldface** type.